A TOUCH OF THE
UNDERWORLD

DR. DAVID TRUCKER

authorHOUSE®

AuthorHouse™
1663 Liberty Drive
Bloomington, IN 47403
www.authorhouse.com
Phone: 1-800-839-8640

Published by AuthorHouse   01/05/2015

ISBN: 978-1-4969-6230-0 (sc)
ISBN: 978-1-4969-6231-7 (hc)
ISBN: 978-1-4969-6229-4 (e)

Library of Congress Control Number: 2014922999

Introduction

The Silent Syndicate, by Hank Messick, published in 1966 was the masterpiece from which I was able to take a myriad of historical points, enabling me to gather together the bits and pieces of my life and that of my family to put them in a reportable form, and for this I am appreciative.

If the content of the book deviates from veracity, you must remember that I am 85 years old and, in all probability, have an element of dementia, and therefore total and exact objectivity is clouded by mental illness, medications, and too many trips to the bathroom.

Before you judge me as an individual, I wish to call your attention to the American Indian adage: "Do not judge me until you have walked one mile in my moccasin." I personally am asking you to walk five miles in your bare feet before you judge me as a person. Remember, we are all products of our heredity and environment, and in my case, being brainless and fearless did not help.

Chapter One

So how did the Mafia in America start and develop? Initially the Cleveland Syndicate was formed primarily by four guys: Moe Dalitz, Louis Rothkopf, Morris Kleinman, and Sam Tucker, all of whom were geniuses. Waves of immigrants came to Cleveland with the people of Jewish origin being first, then the Italians, followed by the Irish and a few from other nations. A guy named Mark Hanna was considered the boss of the Cleveland outfit initially, and he welcomed and nurtured the immigrants. I remember my relatives talking about Mark Hanna and his great achievements such as developing and funding the Cleveland Opera House, which gave him a like of respectability in the community. He was also a master of combining business with political growth and he did so by any means within the framework of the law in contradiction to the parameter followed by the Syndicate. Hanna had a knack for turning politics into money and my uncle Ray Lamb was in the middle of many of the ventures as both a politician and Finance Director of the City of Cleveland. In retrospect, the political and financial efforts of Hanna put President McKinley in the White House, then subsequently the Ohio Gang put Harding in the White House (not a bad arrangement).

Prohibition was the fuel that fired the Cleveland Syndicate, and alcohol could be obtained by various means and was supposed to be used (in accordance with the law) in the manufacture of everything from antifreeze to hair tonic (laugh on dotted line). The base front business of all alcohol was molasses from the Caribbean. The warehouses in Cleveland held literally hundreds of thousands of gallons of whiskey and alcohol (otherwise known as holy water). The Ohio Gang hopped on to the opportunity, and let's just call it the gravy train.

The Ohio Gang had a religious mission, namely dealing with the protection and bootlegging rackets, along with illegal concessions, establishing immunity from prosecution for others, pardons of convicted criminals and paroles, as well as just about any general graft. Allegedly, Cincinnati was the hub of the distilling industry of Ohio, Kentucky and Indiana. Illinois did its own thing, but Cincinnati took the lion's share of the distillation. The trick was for organized wholesale drug companies to get "B" permits, which would allow one to obtain a certain amount of alcohol from warehouses under the Volstead law. In order to get any amount of the stuff in bulk, one had to "cough-up" 50 to 300,000 bucks, and I've often wondered if any of these expenditures were tax deductible. Immunity from prosecution could be readily purchased, not necessarily in the confessional.

Corruption in the Cincinnati-Newport-Covington Triangle was so prevalent that even the general public came to know it as a natural and normal way of functioning. I'm not sure that it was either sanctifying grace or just plain actual grace that kept the citizens going under the guise that they were living in normal parameters (Catholics will understand the differentiation). My personal hero was Abraham Auerbach, who developed "Million Dollar Hair Tonic" and "Love Me, Dearie" toilet water, both of which could be consumed either straight or on the rocks.

Crooks permeated the Justice System. One trick was to condemn the contents of the warehouses to be unfit for human consumption, confiscate the same and subsequently sell the stuff as "residue" to welcoming buyers for the manufacture and consumption of the resulting product (now you figure that one out). The national and state control by the Ohio Gang was unbelievable. Cleveland obtained a reputation as being a "safe city" for gangsters and, might I add, a place for prayer and contemplation.

My father loved vaudeville and in the process he became acquainted with a famous comedy star, Fanny Brice, whose husband Nicky moved to Cleveland, and thereby the link to my dad via the warehouse business, and you can imagine what was in the warehouses constructed by my father.

Executive Order Number 73 in Cleveland required that the city's safety director be advised in advance by the police vice squad of any raids planned within the city limits. The city's safety director did not have an angelic appointment, and somehow word leaked out prior to any raid so that the accosting parties found only empty warehouses and facilities. Eliot Ness eventually became the safety director, and we will discuss this issue subsequently in this book.

There was no abatement of the Syndicate's activities during the mayoral administrations of either Fred Koehler or Ray T. Miller, and it just so happened that while Ray Miller was mayor of Cleveland my uncle Ray Lamb was the finance director of the City of Cleveland, and it just so happened that they also ran the democratic machine in the City of Cleveland, and soon found out the advantages of working with the Syndicate, a very beneficial, mutual relationship. You might call it a spiritual union as my uncle Ray was supposedly a very spiritual Catholic individual and, of course, that major democratic link extended to the unions which became subsequently a very important connection for both my family and myself.

Now Ray Miller's brother was Don Miller, one of the famous Four Horsemen of Notre Dame fame under Coach Knute Rockne, the founder of the forward pass in football and also the "Hail Mary Pass." It's great to have God on your side, whether you're playing football or politics.

Ray Miller, Ray Lamb and Don Miller were the powerhouses of the Democratic Party during the golden years of the Syndicate expansion. The next prominent mayor of Cleveland was Harold Burton, who brought in Eliot Ness as safety commissioner to clean up the city. Ness had been an alcohol tax treasury agent in Chicago (a story in itself). Ness worked hard but hit a brick wall and, unlike Chicago, the Cleveland Syndicate had roots so deep that even a high wind hurricane could not topple the trees.

In Chicago the leaders were well known, like Scarface Al Capone, a neat target for the Feds, and even his opponent did dumb stuff which put them into a position of being arrested and ultimately convicted. However, the leadership in Cleveland remained obscure, and it was not unusual to find "The Boys" in the first row of the nearby Catholic Church.

Ness targeted the Mayfield Road mob with his efforts, not realizing that the real bosses were hiding behind legitimate businesses, a trick that even works today.

Five years later I was born in 1930, and at that time the real battle for control of corn liquor in Cleveland was in full swing. Those individuals who came from out East to either participate or compete met with most unfortunate demises (God their rest their souls).

A fellow named Remus in Cincinnati was the kingpin there until the ex-circulation manager of the Cleveland Plain Dealer, Thomas McGinty came along. McGinty controlled both the front and back doors of the "business." He had both guts and brains, a great contribution for his type of employment, but he found a niche by sponsoring sports events, which certainly made him appear socially acceptable, just another example of combining the legitimate with the illegitimate, at which Cleveland was the mecca. McGinty made the mistake of getting too close to Fred Rickey, the brother of Branch Rickey, the manager of the St. Louis Cardinals, and due to a financial relationship involving "losing a game," McGinty was convicted and ended up in the Atlanta Federal Penitentiary for 18 months. In the Church we call that a Spiritual Retreat.

Although Ness actually had much to do with the demise of the booze era in Cleveland, it did not stop the entrepreneurs from merely moving outside the borders of Cleveland, where good, clean business could continue to function, and in the process the Boys turned to gambling and racetracks. My dad worked at North Randall and Thistledown as a training jockey, and that was actually his hobby in that he built buildings and warehouses for the Boys.

However, booze had a comeback when there were restrictions locally and regionally pertaining to alcohol, and therefore an actual resurgence of prohibition occurred and developed along community, nationality and religious lines. Local leaders were needed to control and bribe those who were obstructionists, and actually thousands of small breweries were the fuel. Raids by cops were very difficult with so many entities to deal with; however, an even greater factor was quality control with a major issue being that many of the consumers died by drinking rotgut. I remember my dad telling stories of making hard liquor in a bathtub out on a farm in the woods, and apparently many Model T's were smashed after the departing individuals attempted to reach their ultimate destinations, not anticipating that heaven or hell would be the place. However, the Big Boys developed control over the corn sugar market, and therefore the Sugar War developed and a few assassination's occurred along the way (God rest their souls).

Much of the corn liquor was produced in very basic housing occupied by immigrants in the Woodland area of Cleveland. I had an Aunt Mae who came from the Irish section of that region and she sang unusual Irish songs, even when she was sober. Collectively these home breweries produced a huge amount of corn liquor, which was collected and distributed by the Syndicate.

I remember my dad talking about the Lonardo brothers. Joe became the "don". The Lonardos were skilled at eliminating their competitions, aptly called housekeeping. That is how I learned to use a vacuum cleaner (remember that the Hoover Vacuum Company was in Canton). Joe eventually moved to Shaker Heights, with the real estate agent being my Aunt Kitty, the first ultra-successful female in real estate in the United States. So how the hell did that happen to a farm girl with a seventh grade education?

Kathryn Lamb Logan was the most influential and success woman in Cleveland in her era. To me she was Aunt Kitty, and since I repeatedly refer to her, it is important for you to know exactly who she was and how she got there.

Kathryn Lamb had to leave school in the seventh grade when my grandmother died, since her two older brothers, Ray and Dick, were in high school and the boys got the priority. Kitty had to tend to the small vegetable and hobby farm outside the City of Cleveland until the boys were out of high school, and then she pursued her education as a high school graduate only. She did not have the opportunity to go on to college and therefore pursued various jobs as a young adult who married a guy named Claude Logan, who subsequently died a few years later of tuberculosis. Kitty was self-supporting and an entrepreneur and she chose real estate as a venture, starting out with a small company and moving up in the ranks. She demonstrated unusual skills in selling real estate, an area not dominated by women.

About that time the Cleveland Syndicate was rapidly expanding due to the graces of prohibition and a significant migration from Italy and Ireland which had hit Cleveland in literally waves. The Syndicate was of Jewish origin and domination, but the Boys were smart enough to find the most energetic of the immigrants and use them to an art of perfection in pursuing the wants and needs of the Syndicate. Actually, many of the immigrants got rich fast and wanted bigtime housing and that opened the door for Aunt Kitty, who considered the new Shaker Heights as the ideal spot for development, and in conjunction with building magnates they developed the best and most beautiful of all the surrounding communities, and that became Shaker Heights as we know it today. In fact, Shaker Heights became the wealthiest community in the United States, greater than Beverly Hills, California at that time. Kitty was also the first woman driver in the City of Cleveland, and she drove the cops nuts since she used horse and buggy traffic rules when driving her car. Every cop in Cleveland knew her and addressed her as "Mrs. Logan," as they knew of her power and political connections which otherwise may be considered a "spiritual relationship."

I truly loved Aunt Kitty for a myriad of reasons, one of which was that she gave me the opportunity of getting out of my boring home in Akron and the pleasantries of her spacious and beautiful apartment on Shaker Square, where I would actually feel important merely by being present in such an atmosphere. Kitty was not a beautiful woman and in fact she was bent over from osteoporosis of the spine, but when she smiled or talked the whole surrounding world seemed to light up and the Syndicate members loved her. She convinced the chief Syndicate members that they should live in the newly established Shaker Heights, a suburb of Cleveland, and naturally their wealth came with them. She was also behind the development of the Rapid Transit, a rail system between Shaker Heights and the Cleveland Terminal Tower to facilitate the movement of workers back and forth to serve all the ancillary and associated needs of the wealthy people in Shaker Heights.

It is also of interest to note that initially in the development of Shaker Heights she worked in conjunction with a competing real estate firm of the Van Sweringen brothers, who although successful in real estate in Cleveland Heights, became bored with that mode of making a living and instead bought the Chesapeake and Ohio Railroad and gave the entire real estate business of the Heights to Kitty, who soon capitalized on the gift. Shaker Heights soon became the home of any respectable Syndicate member.

Both Aunt Kitty and Uncle Ray lived in luxurious apartments off of Shaker Square, and I do specifically remember a lunch meeting at the Stouffer's Restaurant on the Square to which I accompanied Aunt Kitty for a meeting with one of the Boys. Since she called him Moe, I'm presuming it was Moe Dalitz who arrived in a large sedan with darkened windows from which Moe and two guys stepped out. One accompanied Moe into a back room of the restaurant where the meeting was held and the other guy stood at the front of the car. I do not remember the content of that meeting except for Moe to close the conversation with: "Okay, Kitty, it's a deal."

Chapter Two

The competitors of the Syndicate were the Lonardo brothers, and both of them bit the dust after invitations to play cards (a big deal at that time), so the warning is to be careful of invitations to play cards, especially from friends of your wife.

With the competition out of the way, the third phase of prohibition was ready to roll, namely rum running. First class booze, not rotgut, was coming across Lake Erie. This offered the opportunity for the expansion of the Cleveland Syndicate, a highly organized force that still has a major influence not only in Cleveland but throughout the nation, particularly the central states as well as Arizona, Florida and Nevada.

The first slot machine king in Ohio was Nate Weisenberg, who lasted 20 years before being "taken for a ride." I, the author of this book, was dating the daughter of the slot machine king of my own era until for a freshman prom her driver picked me up in a bulletproof car. I told my parents how heavy the door was and that I couldn't see out the windows, and they responded by sending me off to a boarding school which was in a distant state. By the way, that young lady has been successfully married to the same man for over 50 years, and yours truly has had three wives. Could I have done better?

Not to be outdone, the pinball king moved into the house next door to our home in Akron with his large family. They were and are wonderful people that became our close friends, and that relationship continues to the present time. A disaster occurred when shortly after moving next to our home, the Mafia pushed the father, who was from Assyria (it was a country at that time), out of the business and he died of a heart attack. My parents played an integral role in the raising of that large family and my father (and friends) let the Mafia know that this was a bad move.

The Porrello brothers, not part of the Syndicate, bumped off enough of their competition to become very prosperous in the booze world and move to Shaker Heights. Guess who was their real estate agent?

The first grand council of the Mafia took place at the Hotel Statler in Cleveland on December 5, 1928, two years before I was born. A tipoff led police on a raid of this spiritual meeting and 23 arrests were made, with most of the participants being from out east, namely New York and New Jersey. Needless to say, many parole bonds were needed and my dad's good friend Whiskey Dick

Percoco in Akron was the bondsman, having achieved his fame and fortune in the good old prohibition days.

About this time the Boys in Cleveland were running lean and they decided to hook up with the emerging Mayfield Road Mob. The headquarters for the mob was in a saloon outside the City of Cleveland, and this was considered to be the "social center" of Frank Milano, with whom my father had done business before Frank moved to Mexico. By a series of co-alliances, the Mayfield Road Mob actually became the powerful Cleveland Syndicate, and I remember my father speaking of Big Al Polizzi and Charles Colletti. Frank Milano was chief honcho and I had met his daughter at a party, and although she did not know it, I did have a secret crush on her. She lived in a gated estate on West Hill in Akron, and ultimately married at the St. Sebastian's Catholic Church in Akron. Through one of the bodyguards at the ceremony, I did get in to observe the festivities and stood in the back of the church, actually wanting to see the infamous Frank Milano whom I had never seen before. The situation that eventually developed is of considerable interest in that as Frank Milano left the church following the ceremony, he was intercepted by federal agents and arrested for illegal entry into the United States (he had been out for over three years) and was taken for arraignment to Cleveland, where he very quickly developed a "medical condition" and was subsequently released and returned to Akron in time for the wedding parties that evening. That particular series of events again convinced me that the Boys were smarter than the Feds, particularly when it came to working around the legal system at that time.

I remember my dad stating, after James Porrello was blasted with a shotgun as he was holding lamb chops that he had just purchased for a holiday dinner, Dad stated that he could not eat lamb chops for a year. I also went through a similar period of abstinence from lamb after I returned from working in Afghanistan in 1967. The only meat available was lamb at the U.S. Government staff house where I lived. However, I got over it and today I just wipe the blood off and go to it.

Also as an example of a dichotomy, the remaining Porrello brothers went into a Catholic retreat outside Cleveland but apparently God did not get to them, as they were back in action doing their dirty stuff within months, and shortly thereafter were put away for keeps by you know who (God rest their souls). For you pagans who don't know what a retreat is, that's a time of Catholic prayer and reflection that can last from two to seven days, and I've probably done ten of those things but I'm not sure that they helped me except to remember that the food was good.

The Mayfield Road Mob made a reasonable transition from the bullet to the bribe, and the latter allowed everyone to live a long and prosperous life, including my relatives. I remember my aunt Agnes, Ray's wife, having millions of dollars and yet in a nursing home with dementia she would not spend a penny, since she was sure she was broke. The residual millions of dollars proved to be a major problem in the lives of the survivors. Ray's son Jack Lamb was vice-president of Merrill Lynch in New York when he quit that position to purchase the garbage franchise in Philadelphia for about two million bucks, and then subsequently sold the same a few years later for four million and shortly thereafter developed dementia from alcohol, and this precipitated a chain of most unusual events among the survivors.

Chapter Three

The book "Silent Syndicate" by Hank Messick pointed out that although the Cleveland Syndicate had front organizations, like the Mayfield Road Mob, after the dirty work was done, the participants were content to take their profits and enjoy them and if other individuals got the fame (or infamy) and glory, that was not a major problem for the goal-driven Cleveland Syndicate members who simply did not make the mistakes of their compatriots on the east and west coasts.

According to Alvin Giesey, in 1931 Morris Kleinman was the Al Capone of Cleveland. I do not think that was an appropriate comparison, as Morris Kleinman was head and shoulders above the performance of Al Capone. I remember Morris Kleinman's first name since that was also the last name of Aunt Kitty's apartment mate, who was also the girlfriend of Jimmy Lee, and Jimmy played a key role in my life, especially when I spent 14 months in the Rainbow Hospital in South Euclid, Ohio, a victim of rheumatic heart disease. It does pay to have friends, especially when they pay the bill.

Two-thirds of the illegal booze smuggled in the United States came down the Detroit River, across Lake Erie and into select spots along the shores of Ohio. I can remember my dad telling me stories of observing the unloading of cartons of booze from infamous boats tied up to the docks, both in downtown Cleveland and along the lakeshore outside the city. Obviously the police had been well paid to look the other way.

In the late 1920s, Ben Nadel and Morris Goldman were key figures in the booze trafficking in the greater Cleveland area. However, they met their demise in 1928 when they crossed the line and ended up with 14 bullets in Nadel and 12 in Goldman. I believe this is called "air conditioning" in the underworld.

The Syndicate grew regionally and nationally. In Las Vegas, the Desert Inn was a component for the extension of the Syndicate and the site where my present wife encountered Sammy Davis, Jr. in the gift shop trying on sweaters. Being somewhat outspoken, she offered a loud "no" to his first choice, following which Sammy spent about ten minutes trying on various sweaters until he finally received approval. He kept the last sweater on and said thanks and walked out of the gift shop without paying. Two lessons can be learned from this encounter, the first is that a little Jewish boy does not refute the opinion of a Jewish mama; and also when you own the hotel, you do not have to stop at the cashier's desk.

Actually, the original roots of the Syndicate in Cleveland was control of the laundries, most of which were owned by Chinese immigrants who were easily intimidated by power figures. Also, the Dalitz family knew the laundry business over the years and after generations of service in the laundry world, including Ann Arbor, Michigan, Detroit and Cleveland. However, Cleveland proved to be the most fertile soil for developing and expanding the big bucks associated with protection, and thereby Dalitz built an empire. One of the ingenious concepts and fruitions of Moe Dalitz was to negotiate a contract for his laundries in Detroit with James Hoffa, who represented the unions, and they remained friends until Hoffa "took a drink."

The question is why switch most of one man's attention from profitable laundries to all the illegitimate stuff? Well, the answer is obvious and it's called quick cash and lots of it. Although what was going on in Detroit would fill another book, we will continue to deal primarily with the Cleveland Syndicate.

Moe Dalitz moved to Akron and so did my dad, who was hired by Harvey Firestone to be Firestone's architect, a story in itself. Dad and Harvey did not get along, and therefore Dad opened his own architectural office and began working in the greater Akron area for Moe Dalitz and many of the other underworld individuals, such as

Whiskey Dick Percoco, Vinny Vincagara and many other similar figures. Whiskey Dick ended up being a very important part of my life, and let me just tell you two of the stories. First of all, as the name would indicate, Whiskey Dick became notorious and very profitable during prohibition. After prohibition he opened up a bondsman company on High Street in Akron and became a very good friend and client of my father, who built a beautiful home for Whiskey Dick and his wife in the West Hill part of Akron, Ohio. If I hadn't lived through the experience, I would not have thought that such was possible, but it was three o'clock in the morning when my father received a phone call, origin unknown, and he was asked to come over to the house immediately because there had been an auto accident and there was a head under the dining room table. Thinking this was a prank, my father called Chief Linette of the Akron Police Department, who acknowledged that the accident had occurred and that a convertible at high speed had come down the road which ended in Percoco's front yard. The convertible's front wheels hit the curb, catapulting the two individuals in the back seat into the air, one of whom hit the concrete wall in front of the house, and the second went through the plate glass window and in the process his head was totally decapitated and rolled, and the trunk ended up in the living room and the head rolled under the dining room table. Chief Linette said that the coroner would not remove any of the bodily parts until the chief arrived and he stated that he had been to the site, and needless to say there was major pandemonium in the neighborhood.

I went with Dad to the scene, the content of which I remember vividly to this day. The car was still on its top in the front yard, and both the living and the dead had been removed. Dad and I walked into the front door and I remember a squirt of blood along the wall and mirror, which obviously occurred before the body had landed in the living room, forming a huge pile of blood on the white rug. Under the dining room table was a smaller mat of coagulated blood, and I must admit that I just stood and stared. Mrs. Percoco had come downstairs after the accident, took one look and left the house, never to return. My father built another home for the Percocos.

The next encounter occurred when I was approximately eight years of age and playing touch football in the street and had dislocated my knee, and although nowadays that would be treated on an ambulatory basis, I was placed in bed in the hospital in a cast on the second floor of the St. Thomas Hospital in Akron, Ohio. Across the hall from me was Whiskey Dick's son, who had been in the Second World War and had what we call today posttraumatic syndrome, and was stupidly tear gassed out of his apartment in Akron by the Akron police, resulting in his temporary inability to see and moderate difficulty in breathing and swallowing. Both of his eyes were patched, and therefore I spent two days assisting him and feeding him and being his private duty nurse and since there was no television in those days, much discussion was held, particularly about the Second World War.

I was scheduled to go home on the morning of Thanksgiving and Whiskey Dick told the head nun and my father not to take me home, and from one of his restaurants Whiskey Dick set up a complete buffet on the second floor of St. Thomas Hospital for all of the patients and the nuns. The order of nuns was the Sisters of Charity of St. Augustine, an order into which my younger sister would eventually enter. By the way, after my cast was removed and I was in rehabilitation, Whiskey Dick presented me with a new bicycle to assist in the rehabilitation process. You might now see why these individuals were very important in my life and the fond memories which I retain to this day.

Chapter Four

Back to the history of the development of the Syndicate and eventually the Mafia in America. Moe Dalitz was smart enough to see the benefits of the Jews and the Italians working together, and it really paid off. This was especially profitable in the relationship with the Mayfield Road Mob, which eventually became the Syndicate and many of the offshoots became known as the Mafia. The Boys were smart enough to turn garbage into roses at every turn of the road.

So what is the difference between the Syndicate and the Mafia? First of all, the Syndicate members make the big money in illegal activities but fund their families in multiple legitimate businesses and since oil and holy water don't mix, one does not pollute the other. The Mafia functioned as a family affair with all members asked to participate and share in the dirty work and this makes the Mafia much more visible and vulnerable – not a good move.

The guy that established the relationship between the Cleveland Syndicate and the New York Mob was Louis Rothkopf of Cleveland, who was a master at developing distilleries. This opened the door out East to Frank Costello and a spiritual relationship developed.

The connection between the American and Canadian underworld was called "the combination." A creative concept, and it worked. Shipments between the countries and throughout the USA were labeled "Auto Parts." Since Detroit was the disembarkation point, this made sense. Most of the Auto Parts were shipped in boxcars on the Chesapeake and Ohio Railroad, which was owned by the Van Sweringen brothers, the very ones who gave the real estate market of Shaker Heights to Aunt Kitty to go on to bigger and better things. The Cleveland Syndicate and the Chesapeake and Ohio Railroad worked together, and the Van Sweringens bought other regional railroads, but in the long run the business venture did not prove profitable and disintegrated.

Windsor, Ontario Canada was the gateway of booze to America. It went in several different directions. The Eastern Syndicate was formed in New York, New Jersey, Philadelphia and Boston. After an assassination shakedown, the conglomerate became known as the Eastern Syndicate, which functioned more like the Mafia than the Cleveland Syndicate. Names like Meyer Lansky, Bugsy Siegel, Waxey Wexler, Joe Adonis, Lucky Luciano, Frank Costello and Dutch Schultz all became major players and were occasionally seen in church, usually in the front row. The New York Mafia was only a segment of the New York Mob, which had political connections with occasionally religious attachments (this is how I plan on getting to heaven). All of these birds dealt with multiple Canadian distilleries, most of which were under the domain of Distillers Corporation-Seagrams, Ltd. (an organization that survives to this day). Smart gangsters could function reasonably well within the framework of the law (as many do today), and I think they call them "politicians." When the National Syndicate was formed, the Reinfeld Syndicate controlled the East and the Cleveland Syndicate the Midwest, but the Cleveland Syndicate connections in Arizona were gradually developed by the Cleveland Syndicate and were to assume a very major role in the future.

I can remember my dad talking about watching the unloading of booze from boats off the 58th Street dock in Cleveland at night, and I often wonder how he knew the boats would be at that site? Ninth Street was also mentioned, but that would be right under the noses of the Cleveland Police Department – another interesting issue. I literally have tears in my eyes when I read and hear of the hundreds of gallons of good whiskey that either went down to the bottom of Lake Erie or was confiscated by the authorities. I'll bet the politicians and cops had some great parties, particularly with the 2,000 cases of booze that was seized from the Sambo rum running boat alone.

The greatest blessing to the booze rum running was the fact that many of the federal agents assigned to stop the flow of liquor across Lake Erie became corrupt. What a blessing – we call it "conversion" but I can't remember which religions were involved.

The Syndicate and Mafia ultimately emerged in Cleveland, becoming a very powerful political and economic entity. The Syndicate operations were more covert than the Mafia, and the Syndicate appeared to have the brains and the Mayfield Road Mob the guts. The trick was to keep either from being spilled out on the street in blood, and both entities did an excellent job in the greater Cleveland area.

Beer was also a choice item. In November of 1929 on Merwin Avenue in Cleveland, 18 1,000-gallon vats were seized by the Feds, and this apparently was miniscule compared to the several other seizures that were successors. One was on Furnace Street in Akron, and I remember my dad talking about that particular one with a smile on his face. 35,000 cases a month were distributed to target markets in northern Ohio, and the Hollenden Hotel in Cleveland continued to be the Headquarters, which then eventually moved to the Mayfield Road site.

I remember hearing of "Akron Mary" long after she was gone. She ran a high class speakeasy which was well known to Akron politicians and police. The booze flowed freely and was cheap, to the joy of all. Also the Harvard Club was an overt Syndicate operation that soon drew the attention of Eliot Ness and after several changes of location, the facility was ultimately closed (good job, Eliot).

Chapter Five

The Syndicate leaders of Cleveland were notorious for avoiding any convictions except for Morris Kleinman, who got canned for tax evasion. Other characters who weren't so smooth were guys like Al Capone and Waxey Gordon, and you know what happened to them.

The Mayfield Road Mob saw the end of prohibition to be inevitable and began to focus on gambling. A key figure in that racket was "Big A" Polizzi. He was a friend of the Milanos and other powerful Mafia leaders. Frank Milano ran a speakeasy on Lexington Avenue in Cleveland, and Polizzi put Milano out of business (what a friend). About the same time two thugs from Philadelphia bit the dust under unusual circumstances (don't tread on me), Tony and Frank Milano moved to Mayfield Road and opened a headquarters and beer parlor (take your choice) and Coletti, who had joined the Mayfield Road Gang, spun off into the slot machine racket, a business which extended down to my generation and friends.

A great trick of a gangster's was to take similar names plus nicknames and only God could tell them apart. A next tool was to call a "friend" and "cousin" and that truly confused the Feds. Multiple birth certificates were a great ploy, especially to confuse the police and IRS.

The Woodland area of Cleveland was the melting pot of the refugees of Jewish, Italian and Irish origin, in just that order. As they respectively (and non-respectively) made their entrance into big money, they became the "customers" of my aunt Kitty in the real estate world, otherwise known as manna from heaven.

Chuck Polizzi was actually Jewish, as were also the powerhouse figures of Sam Tucker, Moe Dalitz and Louis Rothkopf. Being Jewish with an Italian name was called a "cultural link" and could also be considered a spiritual connection.

The Buckeye Enterprises Company was a "formal arrangement" between the Cleveland Syndicate and the Mayfield Road Mob. Frank Joiner was both an intruder and opponent of the combination, and was found buried head down in a lime pit. Luckily his foot was sticking out, so at least a spiritual service could be held after the body was found. He had tried to muscle his way into the slot machine racket (not a healthy maneuver).

The principle operation of the Buckeye Enterprises was the plush casino in Maple Heights outside of Cleveland. This led to the Beverly Hills Casino in Newport, Kentucky.

Casinos in Cleveland were often listed as offshoots of the Superior Catering Company (depends on what you are catering).

Those who were "in the know" knew that the slots were stored in the Harvard Avenue warehouse (again, Harvard beat out Yale). The Harvard Club was in Newberg Heights. Hiding the gambling business as an "insurance undertaking" was truly an art.

With the Mickey Mouse operations of smuggling out of the way, the emphasis turned to illicit distilleries (now you're cooking with steam). After prohibition ended, the big profit for the underworld was filling the demand for booze before legitimate distilleries could be operational (otherwise known as the open door to heavenly blessings). By 1930 the guys in Cleveland were in full swing and the market exploded to meet the needs of "friends" out East, and this is where the marriage of the Syndicates paid off. No birth control pills were needed in this operation.

Liquor became legal in December 1933 when I was three years old and hitting another type of bottle. The Leader Building in Cleveland was the sanctuary of the operation (praise be to God). Many of the government officials actually worked with the Syndicate (you could call it cooperation). Meyer Lansky and Bugsy Siegel put together the "Bugs and Meyer Mob," which was actually a prayer group (bring your own rosary). The Fischer Brothers Company of Cleveland was more than fruits and vegetables. When Al Capone of Chicago bit the dust,

Sammy Haas of Cleveland rose to the occasion and held a great prayer revival, with again, holy water flowing freely. Lucky Luciano and Frank Costello joined the party. Their baby, the Molaska Corporation was truly the spearhead of organized crime in America at the time. Ultimately this became the National Syndicate and Molaska's task was to fill the need for spiritual enhancement east of the Rockies.

The narcotic business got started in New York, but did not have the national appeal that booze did at that point in time. The pharmaceutical companies had not come onto the scene yet, and that is the move that has truly accelerated the availability and enhancement of narcotics in America (to be discussed in a subsequent publication).

After the Cleveland rum running days were over, the main source of booze was Nassau in the Bahamas, from which the stuff was shipped to Brooklyn and Charleston, South Carolina. Murder Incorporated was a religious organization developed to "treat the apostate." No prayer book was needed. The Boys were not cheap and 30,000 would do the job for whoever you wanted "taken care of," and occasionally a plenary indulgence was attached.

The New Haven Railroad hauled so much booze that the fumes negated the need for coal for the engine– six boxcars with 870 cases per car.

The laundry business in Detroit was a great front. It was amazing how clean all the shirts came out, particularly after all the blood stains had been removed, for an extra charge, of course.

If you wonder why so many of the booze makers' companies were a version of molasses, that is because molasses was used to make the booze. A lot of it came from Cuba in the form of cane sugar. An effort was made to import readymade booze from Belgium, but it didn't pay off so ultimately molasses was the only import of significance that could make quality booze from sugarcane molasses, in a significant amount.

The crooks were smarter than the Feds (isn't that interesting). The fed agencies were totally disconnected and major efforts were required to protect the interests of President Harding, who was actually put in office, both directly and indirectly, by the Cleveland Syndicate. Allegedly Johnny Torrio had been a big Boss in Chicago, but turned that operation over to Capone and moved to New York and found a legitimate operation called Prendergast (even I remember that one). He was one smart cookie and he knew how to get the job done. A new plan in Cleveland to make dehydrated molasses was a major accomplishment and component of the booze making process. The Molaska Corporation was the big screen, and I can remember my relatives talking about the Hollenden Hotel in Cleveland, where many of the underworld meetings were held and the name "Molaska" kept coming up. The Hollenden was considered by many in the underworld to be the "convent or monastery" of Cleveland (religious garb not required).

Chapter Six

"Operation Front" was what outpaced the Feds. With the changes of names and occupations, it was hard to tell who the hell was who or what. I personally knew a couple guys who had three names.

The multiple Molaska Corporations were the sugar sources for the manufacturing of alcohol of all types. The Ray Coal Company (not related to my family) was the front for distilleries, as coal was necessary to heat the pots to make the holy water. Molaska and Ray Coal were good friends, in prayer of course.

The New York money got involved in the "business" in Ohio, particularly Cleveland, and Meyer Lansky was the conduit. Molasses was considered to be like "flowing gold." This was the same Lansky of the Bugs and Meyer mob, and they had connections all along the east coast and extending into Cuba, were Batista eventually became a major player in the liquid gold. Dried molasses, a real step forward, became a priority agricultural product.

When the gangs got in difficulty with the Feds on laundry corruption, the smart guys switched to booze. Who the hell wants to worry about clean underwear when holy water was the priority? Capone was in prison, so he learned the hard way. Some of the key witnesses in the Capone case had been his former allies who turned against him, and Capone got the rap and the other guys slid into the sunset.

Now I don't want you to think that Al was all bad, and I think it's only fair to give the honor and respect to him that he is due and to demonstrate his contributions to American Society, of which I feel the following is the greatest of his spiritual gifts: Only hours after Pearl Harbor's disaster on December 7, 1941, President Franklin D. Roosevelt, a severe polio victim, found himself and the Secret Service in a mess. He was to give the famous "Day of Infamy" speech but there was no way to get him to the joint session of congress. A safe mechanism of transport could not be found. However, one of the Secret Service guys remembered that the U.S. Treasury had seized the bulletproof car of good ole Al Capone. It had been resting in peace in a federal garage since 1931, when I was one year old. I do remember this in between wetting my pants.

Well, it took an armada of workers to get the damn thing ready, but they did it. The floating fort was a 1928 Cadillac, V-8, town sedan. They kept the original black/green colors which had simulated the Chicago Police Department. It had 3,000 pounds of armor (more than my old girlfriend), and inch-thick bulletproof windows that made everything look good. It had a siren and flashing red lights behind the grill and a machine gun mounted over the engine and pointing out the grill. Also there was a jug in the back seat, initially thought to be holy water, but later proven to be a urinal. So the setup was complete to transfer the president after only a tune-up and polish-up job. Al had certainly done his part for American Society.

Many of the operations shifted from Cleveland to Elizabeth, New Jersey when the heat was on. Also, many of the Big Boys changed their names when they had children so they could sit in the front row at church and even the pastor would be confused. If it was a priest, he would pretend that he did not see them.

A major covert operation was held in the old warehouse at 53rd and Sweeney in Cleveland, totally disguised. But the king of king of all booze producing operations was at the border of Akron and Cuyahoga Falls, where I grew up, where a functioning dairy opened (a milk producing plant) on the top level, and the two floors underground produced thousands of gallons of alcohol per day. The whole operation looked like a parade of "milk trucks and tankers" with an unusual smell coming out of the multiple chimneys, and the cops and politicians had to be deaf, dumb and blind not to know what was going on. Many years later I rode my bicycle on the rubble that remained.

A federal agent named Bridges tried to buck the system but he made the wrong moves, as he ran into nothing but brick walls. His successor was our old friend, Eliot Ness, of Untouchable fame who grew up in Roselawn, a suburb of Chicago, the son of a baker, and I had visited the old bakery building with the name "Ness Bakery" engraved in the stone above the door.

As even first graders in Ohio were able to figure out, if you see yellow icicles on a building, it's probably a distillery and not a dog peeing on them. A great trick was to use a gas station as the disembarkation point, where the gas supply tankers were actually hauling away thousands of gallons of booze. The distillery at 5301 Sweeney Avenue in Cleveland could produce over 2,000 gallons of holy water daily. The brewers were masters of stealing all the water, electricity and venting systems needed from other operations to keep the distilleries going. It's called cooperation with unsuspecting partners.

The Baltic Feed Company in Zanesville, Ohio was another front, but it didn't last very long as the Boys were not too smart. A pottery plant in the same town became much more ideal for the operation, but that also did not last long compared to the Cleveland operations. Actually, the Zanesville, Ohio operation was the largest illicit distillery ever seen in American, with 36,506 gallons of mash produced per day (this sure beats corn meal mush). The distillery produced 5,000 gallons of 190-proof alcohol every 24 hours, and this was the best you could get in quality, and therefore the demand was unlimited.

The cost to a buyer was $2.00 per gallon wholesale, therefore up to $2.50 per quart retail. Since the cost to produce the stuff was about $0.50 per gallon, you could just imagine the profit margin. The construction and production of the covert distilleries defied human conception or imagination and beer could be produced at a rate of 36,506 gallons a day.

Chagrin Falls, a suburb of Cleveland, was the home of many of the "Boys" and I remember meeting with several of these interesting characters when I was at the Chagrin Valley Country Club with my uncle Ray. I remember hearing some names like Moe, Sambo, Fingers, Waxey and Bugs.

Chapter Seven

Elizabethville, New Jersey became the new site for development, as much of the underworld in that location was highly experienced and polished in covert operations, and illicit booze was no exception. Woodland Avenue in Cleveland was an embarkation point and, in fact, two of my shirttail relatives from Ireland started out on Woodland Avenue, and many of the Syndicate leaders from that area were related one way or the other. They were all very accomplished at setting up legitimate family businesses and to this day I remain devoted to those individuals and businesses that interfaced with and were most gracious to my family members and myself.

Getting back to Elizabethville, New Jersey, this proved to be the site of easy access and transportation of molasses from Cuba, the basic product being sugarcane. Batista was on the take and very happy with the result, and various feed companies were used as the conduit. This kept the Feds totally confused, plus the fact that the Boys continued to change both their names and the names of their respective companies.

The Beth Realty Company was a predecessor to my aunt Kitty's firm, which ultimately became known as Kathryn Lamb Logan Real Estate in Cleveland, she being first ultra-successful woman in real estate in the United States and the first woman driver in the City of Cleveland, as we have previously discussed. Aunt Kitty literally built Shaker Heights into the mecca of money and gangsters that at the time became the wealthiest city in the United States, per capita, and to this day is still a lovely place to live, if you can afford it.

Going back to the booze world, a real bonanza occurred when a system was developed for converting liquid molasses into a powder form in that the latter was much easier to transport and hide. It was the same technology that was used for making powdered milk, and this was just another reason for disguising the booze business with that of the dairy world. It was amazing how many front door dairies were back doors to distilleries.

When the Molaska Corporation of Cleveland went bankrupt (certainly destined to rise again), some friends of Frank Costello eventually took over the lease, and after a bunch of the Boys in Buckeye Enterprises each planned a loss for income tax purposes, guess what rose out of the cemetery, the good old Molaska Corporation. Actually, in the so-called bankruptcy and liquidation process, distilleries were simply not mentioned in the report to the IRS (truly a lapse of memory).

The Molaska Company passed back and forth, like diarrhea through a tin sieve, and the Feds had a great time trying to figure out which way things were flowing. Constipation was not the problem and, like Patrick Henry said: "Constipation without representation is tyranny." Also, there seemed to be many members of the Syndicate whose changing names made endless headaches for the Feds.

One would notice the expense of "creamery" on many of the expenditures for tax purposes, and of interest was the fact that several of the distilleries were built under creameries (I'll bet that was great ice cream), and the resulting product really had a kick.

Members of the Cleveland Syndicate eventually had interest in the Stardust Hotel in Las Vegas. Further information on the Stardust became recognized by the general public, namely that the Rat Pack controlled the Joint, and this was the first major input of Hollywood stars into the Las Vegas scene, actually before the entertainment phase became the big thing. Also, the owners of the Stardust were alleged to have connections with the Capone Syndicate and other ventures, and many other celebrities were involved.

Chapter Eight

After the repeal of prohibition, illegal booze still flowed under various covers and titles, and wouldn't you know our old friend the Molaska Company resurfaced in many of the larger cities (I'll bet you never knew that molasses could be so important). The question arose, and the Feds couldn't figure it out, how could anyone use so much molasses? Cleveland remained the Hub with allegedly the main storage plant at the railway terminal warehouse on Croton Avenue. Even my dad knew about the location. Booze was available and being made everywhere, from formal distilleries to bathtubs. I remember my dad telling the story of a great party out in the country where the booze was made in the bathtub (of questionable quality) and all the participants were well soused upon leaving the premises. My dad observed two guys spending 20 minutes hugging and shaking hands before leaving and ultimately going to their respective Model T Fords parked at a 90-degree angle around the corner and both took off simultaneously in high gear, literally cementing the front of each vehicle upon impact. The participants survived and hilarious laughter was elicited from all the observers.

Canning plants (which were supposed to be for vegetables) were sites where drums of alcohol were reduced to five-gallon cans. The trick was to keep the canning plants on the move. The wholesale price of booze in New York, Cleveland and Chicago was $2.00 a gallon and the "stuff" could be bought for about $2.50 a gallon (how's that for a deal). The old Diamond-T trucks were used to haul the stuff, and the Diamond-T garage was on 18th Street and it was considered to be the purgatory of the fleet where the trucks were either cleaned up for further use or sent on to truck heaven. I had a shirttail aunt named Mae Cunningham from the Collinwood part of Cleveland who knew Maxie Diamond, and I later learned that he was a member of the Mayfield Road Gang, and she referred to him as Maxie but he was not related to "Legs" Diamond of New York fame.

There was actually a big difference between organized crime in New York and Cleveland. The New York guys were disorganized and not necessarily brilliant. The Cleveland guys were both smart and well organized and much sharper than the Feds (so what has changed).

The unions, beginning in Cleveland and Detroit, worked with organized crime and my father worked for both. To this day I still maintain admiration and a relationship with the unions and organized crime, so at least one can say that I am consistent.

Now, the Cleveland Boys even paid their bills by check and kept records, whereas Al Capone didn't even know how to write a check. So it's not hard to see why the Feds directed their efforts toward the Chicago operation. Also, the Chicago gang had a hind-tit distribution center in Kansas City, but it was operated like kindergarten and, as would be expected, it didn't last.

The Cleveland Boys danced around the law until they hit the brick wall of the Alcohol Tax Unit, a group of the Feds with no consideration of levity, and they couldn't be bought (in contrast with the politicians of today). Subsequently wire taps produced convictions but by paying off the right people, the majority of these were ultimately overturned.

By 1934 the Cleveland Syndicate quit the liquor business as a bigtime deal and turned to gambling, and they weren't even American Indians or the Cleveland Indians, of which the latter's owners remained friends of my family today.

I subsequently found out that the ruins of the dairy above the giant distillery in Cuyahoga Falls (where I rode my bike) had been known as the Liberty Ice Cream Company. Somehow they needed tons of molasses to make the ice cream.

Cleveland in the 1930s was the only city where the police chief drove to work in a Rolls Royce, and it wasn't rented. I actually know where the vehicle came from and I'm convinced that I am in the wrong business.

Now, bookies in the greater Cleveland area paid the Syndicate 100 bucks a week for protection (I would have done it for 75). Mayor Burton had appointed Eliot Ness to the job of safety director (no wonder I felt safe as a kid). Actually, Burton and Ness cleaned up the city so naturally the Syndicate operation moved to the suburbs and set up joints like the Thomas and Harvard Clubs (and you didn't need a degree to get in). Although the TV program the Untouchables presented Ness as a fearless fighter, the Harvard Club is just one example of how he got his ass flogged, kicked and tossed out in one of his fearless ventures. I had a true advantage over Ness, since I was not only fearless but also brainless (now you match that).

When Dutch Schultz got bumped-off at the Palace Chophouse in Newark, New Jersey, the Cleveland Syndicate took the opportunity to expand. Cincinnati was a chosen fleshpot. As law enforcement became more disorganized, the geniuses of organized crime thrived. Lucky Luciano and Frank Costello were the brains of the expansion, and they made very few mistakes.

In 1934 the Boys decided that true success would lie in the development of a national association, and the Salvation Army was not the answer. Slots, narcotics, prostitution, numbers and the garment industry were the emphasis. The Cleveland Syndicate gained control of the entire Midwest except for Chicago, where the thugs of Capone's gang held on, and they were not known for their brilliance. In the allotment of the nation, the Cleveland Boys got Arizona (truly a brilliant move), as the Mexican border sure as hell beat the Chicago suburbs with Chicago bordering on corn and milk country and the Mexican border opening up a whole new world of opportunity, plus the beginning of narcotics. Moey Davis became the "big daddy" in Cleveland, and I remember hearing that name at the Chagrin Valley Country Club when I was with my uncle Ray sitting at a table, and after they'd had a few drinks they were discussing business, and I can assure you they were not saying the rosary. Actually, Moey Davis was Moe Dalitz, one of the original kingpins and geniuses of the Cleveland Syndicate, and my historic hero.

Now, casinos are truly God-sent because they amuse and take money from the rich and employ the poor. Since I am a socialist that works well. It actually took the Kefauver committee to figure out that the Cleveland Syndicate thrived by spreading out its wealth and responsibility to multiple local lieutenants. I had the honor and privilege of knowing several of the children of those lieutenants, and they were not chicken-feed.

Chapter Nine

"Big Al" Polizzi focused on Arizona, and he was smart enough to realize the potential of being on the Mexican border, and he wasn't looking for guacamole. Out East was a guy named Dutch Schultz and he had an overall role and relationship to whomever was somewhat questionable, but he did have a working connection with the Cleveland Syndicate. Although Dutch was from out east, he made a move into Cincinnati, part of Cleveland's turf (not a healthy move), and he eventually paid the price for that bit of indiscretion. For those not familiar with his demise, Dutch was having a meeting with his gang in the Chophouse when the visitors in long, black coats came in and decorated the room with machinegun fire. Dutch was actually in the bathroom, an appropriate place to take a shower from machinegun fire. One of the victims at the table was eating spaghetti, and the lesson to be learned from this situation is never to shoot anybody who is eating spaghetti because when the press comes later to take the pictures of the crime scene, it is not aesthetic to see spaghetti hanging out of someone's mouth.

Big profits from prohibition in both the United States and Canada actually dumped large amounts of money into various American enterprises like horse and dog racing. The Syndicate in Cleveland developed North Randall and Thistledown tracks, where my father worked part time training racehorses, and this was actually his hobby since he was an architect for the Boys. Dad was paid very well for doing very little at the tracks, and since he was single at the time, this was a neat place to go and relax and play with the horses when he wasn't building homes and businesses for the Boys. Remember, the Amish do not discriminate and since he was of Anabaptist origin, at no time did he attempt to judge the people by whom he was employed.

Horseracing proved to be much more durable than dog tracks, and evidence of that fiasco exists two miles from my present home in Hudson, Wisconsin, where a magnificent structure and vacant property sit empty and unclaimed, and as I pass it frequently I just shake my head, acknowledging the wrong thing at the wrong time and a hell of a bad decision.

Now Dutch Schultz's payoff guy was a fellow named Abbadabba, and I loved the name, which really stuck, even when I was a kid. The guy was supposed to be a genius, but I also was supposed to be one (I wonder what happened). Reportedly, Abbadabba was one of the guys that got bumped off in the Chophouse, truly a waste of talent.

The next fun thing on the horizon was slot machines, and it just so happened in high school I was dating a lovely young lady who was the daughter of the slot machine king in Ohio. As I said before, things were going well until I told my parents that we went to the prom in a bulletproof car, where the door was so heavy I could hardly close it. That ended that relationship, not by my choice.

The next minor initiative in the so-called underworld was the pinball machine racket, and this actually got started because music was played when you put your dime into the pinball machine, along with all the other stuff bouncing around, and as you may remember, the Syndicate was intimately involved in the music industry. As I stated before, it just so happened that next to my home in Cuyahoga Falls, a wonderful family moved in with many young children. The father had managed to become the figurehead of the pinball machine move in Ohio, but was forced out of the business by the Mafia, a situation which produced severe stress, a heart attack and death, on a day which I still remember vividly, and following which my parents took an active role in assisting the family with an enduring relationship which exists to this day. This is merely an example of the sustained relationship and assistance which exists among members of the underworld.

Numbers actually became a big deal and continues today in legitimized forms in various states. Even the nuns in my sister's order love to gamble. I really don't know what happens if one of them wins.

When the National Syndicate had formed, the Boys were smart enough to leave Dutch out, and that was probably because of his intrusion into the Cincinnati area. This exclusion made Dutch vulnerable to misfortune, which did occur, as above described. In essence, his shield was gone. But prior to his demise he retained the Coney Island Racetrack in Cincinnati, but he actually did not know how to make it profitable or even run it as a façade.

The execution of Dutch Schultz on October 23, 1935 at the Palace Chophouse in Newark, along with his associate Abbadabba, opened considerable speculation. Rumor had it that Dutch was bumped off to prevent his killing of the then New York District Attorney Thomas Dewey (remember that name?). Dewey was destined for big things and this is just another example of where the politicians worked with the Mafia to get the job done. In fact, the killing of Dutch put Murder Incorporated on the map where there was already plenty of blood, actually enough to produce a successful blood donor drive. Being of Catholic origin, I really had to laugh about the fact that Dutch was Jewish but when he was dying in the hospital he called for a Catholic priest. That's known as covering both sides of your ass, since you definitely don't want to get caught in the middle. As to who did the job, I'll put my money on the Cleveland Syndicate, an organization of monastic origin.

Chapter Ten

Is it surprising that after Dutch's death the Coney Island track in Cincinnati had new owners, namely the Cleveland Syndicate, and a new name, River Downs. I was 18 years old at the time and knew of the dealings, but I was busy with my own stuff and issues and didn't even take a trip down to Cincinnati. However, River Downs proved to be a gold mine and the Boys did well. A major investor was Henry Green of New Jersey, and he also worked with the Cleveland Syndicate to develop Thistledown Racetrack in Cleveland, again, my dad's hangout. Then eventually Thistledown was added next door to North Randall, and the two horse tracks together drew tremendous crowds but eventually went through a series of bankruptcies and other roadblocks but were still red hot when I was a teenager.

Horseracing was getting stale and the Syndicate and Green moved on to Las Vegas and were involved in the development of the Desert Inn with the Rat Pack (Dean Martin, Frank Sinatra and Sammy Davis, Jr.). Again, my present wife was a frequent flyer at that facility, but it's amazing that she never paid a penny for any expense from the time she hit the front door until her departure from the same (I guess it pays to be good looking).

Although Cincinnati was known as the most corrupt city in America, one must not overlook the spiritual aspect of the city. I guess it's built on seven hills (like Rome) with a church on every pinnacle, and therefore spirituality interfaced inseparably from corruption, and I wish to point out the 1919 World Series in Cincinnati, which is now known to have been "fixed", and I don't think this was a problem in that "somebody had to win."

When the heat got turned up in Cincy, the Boys moved across the river to Newport, Kentucky, a brilliant decision. The town was wide open and the rewards were endless. At the same time the mob moved into the communications world, establishing the Nationwide News Service, which eventually became the Continental Press. This opened up the door for legitimate businesses, and my relatives bought in bigtime in radio stations in Cleveland and eventually they were the pioneers in television in that city. Communications was very important to the underworld, since that was their mechanism of linking with bookies across the nation.

I was blessed enough to know Alan Freed, the father of rock 'n' roll, when he was a meager disc jockey on WAKR in Akron and before he moved on to WJW in Cleveland, and then subsequently his move to New York.

I really liked the guy but his life went on to tough times, but needless to say rock 'n' roll persisted. I remember when rock 'n' roll could not be used as a term, since it meant "screwing" among the black community, and therefore had to be introduced with a melted down version called "Rhythm 'n' Blues". Actually, rhythm in the Catholic Church meant "timed screwing", so what else has changed?

The Fox and Crow Club in Montgomery, Ohio was a unique venture, combining gambling and food. Now you know where the American Indians got the idea. "Feed –em" and "screw -em" was the motto and it worked. You spend more when your belly is full--- just make sure your belly is not full of buckshot.

"Ding-donging" was the term used to get the local boys on board. Occasionally this required castration, but usually torsion produced the desired result. It's all part of the "menu." My dad built three restaurants in Akron for a guy named Vincigara, and all three were burned down. Some people learn the hard way, but my next question is – do you want to build a restaurant?

The invasion of the Cleveland Syndicate into Arizona was in about 1945 when I was 15 years old. Reportedly Big Al Polizzi wanted to go big game hunting near Nogales, Mexico. That is amusing to me since my first major assignment in the U.S. Army during the Vietnam War was Fort Huachuca, Arizona, about 20 miles from Nogales, the home of my secretary. The only thing the soldiers were hunting in those days were the girls in Nogales and across the border, and I guess you could call that game hunting. Sometimes the guys caught more than the girls, as we had the highest venereal disease rate of all military installations in the United States, and I don't know why I didn't get a medal for treating them.

What a break – the Mexican border, literally a sieve (and it remains that way today). Just think, booze, narcotics and girls. What more could a bigtime gangster want?

The quality of the booze being consumed by the soldiers across the border would definitely be classified as rotgut, and actually one of my jobs at Fort Huachuca was to accompany the hearse across the border to bring back the guys that died in the brothels (what a way to go), or were killed in auto accidents at a single turn on the way back. So as you can see, I did serve valiantly.

However, things became more problematic when the following scenario played out. The sheriff of Cochise County lived in back of me since he was eligible to live on base since his wife was principal of the schools on the base. He came to me one night and said that his deputies assisted a pickup truck near Sierra Vista, and the driver was a soldier and the back of the truck was loaded with cases of booze from Mexico. We agreed to keep our mouths shut, which I always did when I prayed, but two months later the Feds nailed nine MPs from the base for selling illegal booze in the noncommissioned officer's club, a violation of the Federal tax code. They were not kidding in that all nine were convicted and sent to Fort Leavenworth Prison, where I ended up spending some time involuntarily when my military time was extended following my discharge because of medical reasons. During the recovery period I worked in the clinic at Fort Leavenworth and I should have been given a medal for visiting my friends in the prison.

Chapter Eleven

The Eastern and Cleveland Syndicates joined forces in Arizona, realizing the unlimited potential. At this point Big Al Polizzi was recognized as the Ohio Mafia, which was actually an offshoot of the Mayfield Road Mob. What became very important was the fact that Frank Milano, one of the founders of the Mayfield Road Mob, was then living in Mexico and the bridge was wide open. Polizzi and Frank Milano, along with his brother Antonio, had become wealthy during prohibition and were now ready for the next big step.

After four years in reform school (to be discussed in my next book), I had done remarkably well academically and subsequently got a scholarship to John Carroll University, a Jesuit institution, in Cleveland, and that's where I met Angelo Milano, Tony's Nephew. Angelo was only at John Carroll for a year and I did not keep in touch with him after he returned to Italy, which was his primary love. In college I worked harder than the other guys (since I wasn't as smart as they were), and I actually completed all of my requirements for medical school in three years. And because of my endless study hours, I really had no time for social events. Plus the woman that I loved became a nun and so I decided – "to hell with that love stuff."

The Unione Siciliano was called the "Brotherhood", which was the polite term for the Mafia. The Milano Boys were the bosses and they were my heroes in their latter days. I was intrigued with the fact that they were smarter than the Feds.

I was actually only four years old when Frank Milano moved to Vera Cruz, Mexico and started a whole new empire with coffee and lumber. Remember how I said that the Cleveland Boys knew how to set up legitimate businesses in contrast to their competitors? My relatives were geniuses in the political/business world, and many of them were connected directly and indirectly to the Syndicate.

Tony Milano remained in Cleveland and had some connection with my uncle Ray Lamb which I could never figure out. Both of the Milano brothers had multiple covert operations and Lucky Luciano got involved in the game, cultivating the route between Vera Cruz, Mexico and Arizona for the transfer of narcotics. We no longer need that transit route since we have the pharmaceutical industry enabling the distribution of narcotics through allegedly legitimate medical channels (are we stupid or not?). A key site was the Grace Ranch near Tucson. I'm not sure whether the Grace was sanctifying or actual (a Catholic joke), but the Joint was a hotspot and a key hub of operations. The cattle were invisible (a new breed), but could be seen at night with a microscope, so the ranch was legit.

I never have been able to figure out how a guy from Russia picked up the name of Thomas Jefferson McGinty, but who am I to judge the angels and the saints? Somehow McGinty got hooked up with the Cleveland Syndicate and thus developed successful casino operations in the greater Miami region. Since Meyer Lansky was involved, obviously the operation was a joint venture of the Cleveland and Eastern Syndicates, and the Boys were smart enough and knew how to get along, except for the Chicago group and our old friend Capone. McGinty was the boss of the Irish faction in Cleveland, which had recently arrived in Cleveland and were very welcomed immigrants, some of whom were my shirttail relatives. I hadn't realized that the Irish came from Russia until I heard about that McGinty guy.

When prohibition ended, gambling was the key enterprise and proved to be highly profitable. I loved the concept of "betters" being classified as "contributors" in the gambling casinos before the whole thing became legit. By being called "contributors" the winners could be classified as receiving "dividends," but the Feds didn't buy that one. But they were confused for long enough time to fill the coffers plus the pride and joy of all the participants, winners and the Syndicate. In 1933, Ohio legalized parimutuel betting and the term "contributions" was out the window. This was the time when horseracing was in its prime and my father was reaping the benefits.

However, new angles had to be developed and therefore prizefighting, bicycle races and roller derbies hit the scene, all of which could be fixed for a price. As we all know, fraud in bicycle racing exists today but roller derbies were of interest to me. A classmate of mine in grade school went on to national fame in roller skating and was one of the founders of the concept of roller derbies, and he stated to me very specifically that payoffs and bribes could be utilized with considerable profits accompanying an incident or accident. By falling, one could reduce his or her betting rating from first to last and the coffers could be cleaned by the Boys. Also the sport was fun to watch when girls were the participants (wow).

Now back to our friend McGinty. He was very clever and it took several tries before Eliot Ness could bust his well-concealed joint in the Hotel Hermitage. McGinty worked out a compromise with the Syndicate on the control of Thistledown Racetrack, and so the Russian/Irishmen learned to run with the pack.

The new Mounds Club in Lake County was a huge success, adding entertainment to the food and gambling. This is just another example stolen eventually by the American Indians and their current casinos. McGinty also got involved in the Desert Inn in Las Vegas and eventually spread his wings to Havana, and guess who was lounging in Havana? – Meyer Lansky, working with Batista, who was called "The Sergeant" because of his strict rule in Cuba.

Chapter Twelve

In case I've overlooked the importance of the Hollenden Hotel in Cleveland, I knew it well. I was with Aunt Kitty there for a meeting with two guys who were surrounded by four bodyguards. I thought it was kind of exciting and I spent my time talking to one of the guards who had a weird accent from some God knows country. Later I learned that many of the hoods lived in the hotel, and when I asked if I could stay there for a few days, I was given a cold "no."

The Syndicate was like a military organization with four top generals: Dalitz, Kleinman, Rothkopf and Tucker. They made all the decisions. The work, dirty or clean, was carried out by the lieutenants. Moe Dalitz was the only name I heard my dad mention but Aunt Kitty knew the whole crew.

Empire News became the Ohio branch of the Continental Press. This provided a link for betting all over the nation, a very fortunate and productive link.

Reverse prohibition occurred about 1950 when covert booze operations were directed from the USA to Canada (the chickens came home to roost). I was 20 years old and knew about some of the plans, but I was too busy looking into medical school and wanted to keep my nose clean, not knowing of the bonanza that I would find in Chicago (to be described in my next book).

The booze traffic between Chicago and Toronto was more than profitable. It seemed that the Feds didn't really give a damn, since they were concentrating on tax evasion in the United States, particularly their friend Capone in Chicago. The big base of operations in Chicago was on North Kilpatrick Avenue, and the name itself gives fantasies of good old Irish whiskey, which was a mainstay where I grew up. I also ended up in a reform school with a boy whose parents owned Emmet Imports in Detroit, the organization which had total control of all imports of Irish whiskey (my favorite whiskey to this day). The Canadian connection, both during the legitimate and illegitimate days, was highly tied to an organization which today we call Hiram Walker.

In 1941 I was 11 years old and the Kefauver committee was in full tilt. The Boys had to pull in their wings and many went into legitimate businesses where they were also very successful. For example, in Akron, Whiskey Dick became a bondsman and a good client for my dad and a bountiful friend to myself, particularly when I spent 14 months in the hospital with rheumatic heart disease, having been sent there to die. (I wonder what happened.)

Covington, Kentucky was a gambling mecca, but the crime rate was very low and can you imagine why? Actually, petty criminals were eliminated by the mob, and perhaps that could be the solution to uncontrolled crime in America today, particularly criminals of the Mickey Mouse category.

The Cleveland Syndicate became not only national but also international in scope, with Cuba and Mexico being the first steps. A guy named Tucker was in charge of expansion, and remember, he was one of the generals.

Chapter Thirteen

I have no idea where the idea came from that Eliot Ness was a hero in his role. That's not the story I got. For example, when Ness was Cleveland's safety director (whatever that was) he had an "ace investigator," Lieutenant Ernest Molnar, and in 1939 a grand jury voted indictments which went into a sealed envelope, pending further investigation. Anyway, the contents got "leaked" and the Boys took off on a yacht to Florida, which ultimately ended up at Frank Milano's joint in Vera Cruz, Mexico (now how's that for navigation?). The fact that Molnar was a crook and the source of the leak was known by everyone else except Eliot Ness. The stories of Ness' naïveté are literally mind boggling and overwhelming.

The Boys went to Florida, especially Big Al, and built the City of Coral Gables. See, I told you that they were upstanding citizens – they would stand up anyone they could.

The Second World War opened up new vistas of legitimate and illegitimate contracts and the black market thrived. New York and Washington were the hubs. The story of stories was that naval intelligence needed help from the Mafia to protect the east coast shipping from sabotage. I was aware of this when I applied to the Coast Guard Academy at New London, Connecticut, but the war ended and I went into medicine. Lucky Luciano took over my "tasks" on the east coast, and probably did a better job. Now if you believe that one, I have land to sell you in Bagdad, however, bear in mind that Luciano did part of his job in the Mafia during his 50-year sentence. After he was released, Lucky ended up in Vera Cruz, Mexico with his old friends Meyer Lansky and Frank Milano (this is truly the alternative to paradise).

Many of the Boys were born in Russia and were of Jewish ethnicity and all were brilliant businessmen and knew when, where and how to get a job done, a principle that I learned from them early in life. Some of the guys had rap sheets a mile long but payoffs were the mode of the day. It really paid off to know the right people.

The next racket was smuggling of gold. Canada had plenty of it, especially out of the Timmins Mine in Ontario. Reportedly over three million bucks per year was "unaccounted for" and in all probability was going to charity. Other legitimate successes by the Boys in the business world could be seen in the example of the Tiptop Brewing Company in Cleveland, a name I well remember. Ohio was the first state to have a monopoly system of liquor licensing and control. So all the permits to sell had to go through the State. Along came the war and a shortage of booze occurred, and this produced an open door system licensed by the state that permitted tavern owners to buy booze from out of state (more manna from heaven). What a great open door for the Boys. You can just guess what subsequently occurred.

Peerless Liquor in Chicago was a smuggler's haven. Polizzi worked his way into being the middleman in this out-of-state transfusion, and both liquor and blood did flow. Our old friend Batista in Cuba also played a role in the conduit of holy water to Ohio. The Cedar Valley Distillery in Wooster, Ohio, the town next to Akron, blended bourbon with less expensive rum from Cuba, and this stuff was marketed as "blended whiskey" which was of poor quality and much different than the blended whiskey on the market today. The tricks were endless, so hold on to not only your wallet but also your teeth, especially if they have gold inlays. I personally will lay next to gold any day. It is interesting to note that needed money for smuggling could be obtained from legitimate business men. My uncle Ray Lamb became the head of the Cleveland office of Merrill-Lynch Stock Brokerage Company, and I remember hearing him mention Batista's name at a social gathering, again at the Chagrin Valley Country Club. My cousin's husband, a famous World War II submarine commander, became his successor. So as you can see, we were not all bad guys. It was the same commander who couldn't figure out why I wanted to go into medicine when I could make millions in the stock brokerage business, and I later learned as an adult that the mechanism that he was describing to me as the road to fame and fortune was literally "inside trading."

Kentucky was the arch-icon in the production of Whiskey and remains so to this day. Their stuff is really the best. Needless to say, the Boys from Cleveland came knocking on the door and when the legitimate channels were at quota, the black market came in handy and in full swing, and believe it or not, part of the funding came from Canada (it's great to have good neighbors). Some of the Boys built up an empire of legal whiskey and with the jacked-up prices they made a fortune. The Office of Price Administration ceiling price was only a starting point. The sky was actually the limit and additional charges were called "overage," a polite term for skimming or screwing. Kentucky became a mecca for whiskey and the big daddies were called Kentucky Colonels, a step down from the generals that I had previously described, but equally as wealthy. A Milwaukee distillery became the bottling plant of much of the stuff from Kentucky that was then transported to Ohio for anxious buyers. Bottling plants in Ohio were not feasible or profitable at the time and were apparently too high profile.

Chapter Fourteen

As stated before, the Mafia really started with the control of laundries in Cleveland, Detroit and New York. That interest persisted since most of the laundries were run by Chinamen of questionable legal status and they had no mechanism to protect themselves. Therefore they were not only an easy prey, but Mickey Mouse gangsters were afraid to rob them because the Mafia would retaliate with unprecedented brutality (I like the idea).

After World War II, Wire-Service became a big deal and a newcomer on the scene was Mickey Cohen. Does that name sound familiar? He and others were involved in a nationwide news service which distributed information on races to bookies (a great idea).

In Chicago, it took the Italian-Jewish-Irish underworld quite a while to learn the potential of working together. Needless to say, the brains came from the Jewish side of the fence and the combined gang turned to Cleveland for help right about the time that Frank and Tony Milano were starting their brotherhood loan company, and with friends like that, who needs a brother?

The next venture was control of cabs in Cleveland, and that was achieved by putting the chief of police on the payroll, and that was a combined venture that I've never been able to figure out, except I did know that the chief drove a Rolls Royce and there were some days on which he even had a chauffeur.

Allegedly a guy named McBride was behind the development of the Cleveland Browns professional football team. But remember that the Cleveland Browns were actually a product of Paul Brown, the famous football coach from Canton/Massillon High School fame, and he achieved that status by having only one high school for the combined two cities of Canton and Massillon, and both of those cities consisted primarily of blue collar and steelworkers. Needless to say the kids were physically little supermen who became national high school football champions year after year (now that was truly ingenious).

Now the Wire-Service went through many hands without any interruptions in service. Capone definitely had both of his hands and feet in the deal and operations became so heated that the kingpin Roger Reagan was riddled on the streets of Chicago. This left the whole operation in limbo because the old boy loitered and lasted seven weeks before biting the dust, and during this time outside fingers came into meddle since his successors had to wait for his demise, which had not been appropriately arranged for.

About this time the National Syndicate split up, with Bugsy Siegel getting California and Meyer Lansky Florida. Controlling the unions in California was critical toward moving forward. However, Bugsy Siegel had a vision for a small community in Nevada called Las Vegas, as it was the right distance from Beverly Hills to get the money suckers to bit, and they did. The Flamingo Hotel was the prototype and the first of many hotels that would make up the strip.

Los Angeles hatched a guy named Dragna, who became the Al Capone of that region. The Wire-Service was the hot button but it got into bigtime trouble. Again the Wire-Service was extremely important because it was the link to and between the bookies all over the nation. This was a whole new profitable industry.

One of the reasons that the Cleveland Mafia was so successful was that the four original founders stayed united for 40 years. Therefore, the names of Dalitz, Kleinman, Rothkopf and Tucker became the icons of the Cleveland Syndicate and all of its offspring, no matter what name you wished to give to the fledglings. As you will notice in this book, literally all of the ventures developed by these four individuals were successful to one degree or another, and when success was not inevitable, they knew when to either bail out or sell.

After the Beverly Hills assassination of Siegel in 1947, a guy named Mickey Cohen took the reins of the California Syndicate and he was a friend of Tony Milano and a few of the other Boys. Actually, Tony Milano moved to L.A. temporarily to assist Mickey in "operations," and he temporarily lived in Cohen's home for a while and this tended to tighten the relationship and network. Another one of the young, frequent visitors to Cohen's empire was "Babe" Triscaro, who eventually became a lieutenant for James Hoffa, the teamster president and, as you are well aware, Jimmy did not end up making all the right moves and paid the consequence of the same. The lesson to be learned from his demise is that when you are burying a body in water, you do not use rope as a restraint, as it eventually corrodes, but instead you resort to more scientific mechanisms such as duct tape or cement blocks, of which the latter is preferred.

Pipelines to Mexico were developed and were profitable. California was an ideal location not only to obtain "stuff," but also to distribute alcohol in many forms. However, in spite of all the national development and division of territory, the Hollenden Hotel in Cleveland remained the headquarters for not only the Cleveland Syndicate but all of the national and international interconnections and communications necessary to keep the entire operation in business and the holy water flowing.

When Luciano escaped to Italy, after his release from the clink, Frank Costello became the new boss of the bay area in 1949. When Las Vegas started to smell good, the

Cleveland Syndicate was quick to appear on the scene ready to lend a helping hand, of course. The Continental Press had been killed by the Kefauver committee, so new vistas had to be pursued.

The Los Angeles Police Department cleaned house (most unusual), and so the Boys had to move out but only a short distance up to Las Vegas, where they continued their prayer sessions (rosaries were not provided).

Chapter Fifteen

Arizona came of age after World War II when the Syndicate rightly predicted a boom in both legitimate and illegitimate business. Licavoli was the link from the Cleveland Syndicate to Arizona. Moey Davis headed the Cleveland operation and was considered to be a key link with the Mafia. Also, Youngstown, Ohio continued to operate overtly and covertly and that continued up to the time when I was the medical director of the workers' compensation system in Ohio, not by choice. As an appointee of Governor Celeste, I readily learned the art of dirty politics. Actually, one of the congressmen from Youngstown ended up in prison even at that time, which was 1985, and believe me, he was a wild one.

One of the legitimate businesses of the Syndicate in Tucson was the Tucson Printing Company which could do both legitimate and illegitimate business. After all, the gaming sheets had to be printed somewhere. As the legit-link, Moe Dalitz also bought the Tucson Steam Laundry, as laundries were always a profitable, legitimate business and Moe had been in the laundry business all his life, even when he was in the U.S. Army. Motels were also a profitable enterprise, e.g., Tucson Hotels.

In real life when things got too hot for the Boys, they would enter a hospital with some fictitious diagnosis or illness, fabricated by a physician functioning on the edge. It worked every time since hospitals were not mental giant institutions at that point in time, and sizable contributions by the "patients" would open the back door if the front door was not felt to be appropriate. The covert nature of most operations resulted in the title of the book: "The Silent Syndicate," the document by Hank Messick in 1966 and the source of much of the information upon which I have expanded and elaborated. In reading the book, I felt that I was actually reliving some of the experiences described.

I had previously described the slot machine empire but it went through many lieutenants, starting with Nate Weisenberg, and again, at my time being under the control of a guy whose daughter I was dating. I was a teenager and puppy love was great. I learned to wag my tail and other anatomic parts.

So what was the story with Nate Weisenberg? Remember that Cleveland Heights is not within the City of Cleveland, so that brings in a whole new scene of characters (as I was to find out a few years later). Nate had lost the back of his head in an execution, and I'm not sure they ever found it. Needless to say, one does need the back of his head to talk to the front of the head, as in some people there is a connection. The car and body were riddled in gangland style, which is conveniently called "a shower."

Investigation revealed that Nate had 69 slot machines well hidden on Chester Avenue in Cleveland, and I think he forgot to tell the Syndicate that he had a side business (not a wise move).

Now back to our old friend Eliot Ness, who was city safety director under Mayor Frank Celebrezze, a close friend of my uncle Ray Lamb. I remember Uncle Ray talking to the mayor at the Chagrin Valley Country Club, but I do not remember the content. Apparently there had been a bigtime meeting of the top Boys and Nate at the Hollenden Hotel on the date he was killed. It was noted that all of the Big Boys lived outside Cleveland, so they were usually not seen in the City of Cleveland after dark except for important meetings.

It was ultimately proven that Weisenberg had a vast empire, including music stores in many cities such as Denver, Phoenix and Tucson. The music business led to jukeboxes that were used to play the music in those days, and then ultimately on to pinball machines and even slot machines that would play various forms of musical notes to either entertain or mesmerize the participants. The music instructor for my oldest son, who had a band in California for 20 years, was the guy who obtained a considerable fortune by developing music for elevators.

A guy named Cadillac Charlie emerged as leader of the lesser ranks of the Mafia, but he was polished off in Youngstown, a town where anyone could be bumped off for a fee. In fact, there were some occasions when a fee was not necessary and merely "good hunting" was the motive.

I was 23 years old, and in medical school, when there was a big stink in Cleveland relative to state offices and the governor's mansion being owned by the Syndicate or members thereof. So what? The Boys had economic stability and that's more than what could be said for the City of Cleveland.

Chapter Sixteen

The legitimate and illegitimate operations in Cleveland were smart enough to work together. My family was the legitimate side of the fence and they had no problem working with the illegits. Probably the greatest illustration was when The Depression hit Cleveland and thousands of laborers and immigrants were out of work. Cleveland was going down the drain when my uncle Ray Lamb, then finance director for the City of Cleveland, and two other ranking democrats went to the Syndicate and asked for money to build the Cleveland Terminal Tower. $68 million was required and the Syndicate provided the cash. The Terminal Tower was supposed to have been financed by the Van Sweringen brothers, who had given their lucrative real estate business to Aunt Kitty when they went into the railroad business, but their tenure as railroad tycoons was short as their multiple railroad ventures did not prove fruitful and they had to back out of their commitment to finance the Terminal Tower. The joint venture between the Syndicate and unions enabled that structure to be built and Cleveland rose like a phoenix from the ashes of The Depression. This project revitalized the economy of Cleveland and to this day the Cleveland Terminal Tower is known as a masterpiece of design and function, being completed in 1928, actually two years before I was born.

The reason that the Cleveland Syndicate worked so well for so long was that all major decisions were shared, and so were the profits, so that one big happy family resulted. I am proud to say that we were part of the "family" and my integral part will be revealed in a later publication.

Laundries kept popping up as Syndicate controlled, and what a better, necessary, enduring and profitable legitimate business could one give to deserving family members? An example was the Pioneer Linen and Laundry Company, where contracts with hotels and restaurants were a guaranteed profitable bonanza. One of my best friends while growing up was one of those giants, so it pays to keep your nose and laundry clean. The list of legitimate companies and corporations into which the Syndicate had ownership was a mile long. I knew a few of them, but had no idea of the owners. One of the hidden gems of the time was Drive-In Theaters, the place where most of us learned to make love and whoopee and a few other things. Another corner on the market was that of bondsmen. Whiskey Dick owned a bonding company on High Street in Akron and my dad told me that no one ever got away without repaying the loan and interest, and the few that did not – may they rest in peace.

The Cleveland Arena was another deal that became the home of the Cleveland Hockey Company, later called the Cleveland Arena, which I had visited on many occasions. Also I well remember the Brady Lake Amusement Park with all its rides and stuff, but I did not know at the time that there was an attached casino through a narrow door in the back of the park into a building that looked like a small warehouse. It was probably just a spot for prayer and reflection. When I ate at Lindy's Restaurant on Euclid Avenue in Cleveland, I had no idea it was a hotspot. I guess the gambling was in the back room where the swinging door had considerable traffic. As a 16 year old, I was only interested in the food and my uncle paying for it.

The Cleveland Syndicate members were masters for providing employment for their relatives and kids. It was my pleasure to know some of those kids but I prefer not to give their names so as not to intimidate or embarrass those wonderful friends and/or their family members.

My older cousin Jack took me to the Roxy's Burlesque on Ninth Street and he got me in because he knew the doorman, even though I was definitely underage. That was truly great stuff to watch and my testosterone and other anatomical parts went up.

Chagrin Falls and Chardon became the hub of the Syndicate because of the Chagrin Valley Country Club, where my relatives belonged, plus many of the Boys lived out that way and some of their families still do. I have a sister, three years older than myself, a retired nun at the mother house in Chardon, and over the years and to this day she is well familiar with many of the members of the Syndicate and their families plus a few of the Boys who drifted off into the realm of the Mafia and paid the penalty for so doing. The Chardon-Chagrin area is beautiful and hilly. Since most of eastern Ohio is flat, that region is a choice site for home development, plus it's easier to hide in the hills and Rothkopf's living there gave prestige to the area.

Dayton, Ohio tried to become a mecca but it lacked the spirituality and pooped out under the pressure from the press. Obviously the right people were not paid off.

The laugh of the century was that booze was illegal in West Virginia, so obviously no one had taken a ride up into the hills. Even I knew where the joints were outside of Huntington, West Virginia, and actually local officials and citizens ignored the law since they loved the joints, which meant both entertainment and economic prosperity.

Chapter Seventeen

The Syndicate had a neat system of having a different "corporation" owned various segments of any operation, and this was totally confusing to the Feds. As an example, relative to a specific piece of property, the building would be under one corporation and the restaurant, casino, porta-potties and other entities would all be under different and separate corporations. I opted for the porta-potties, as that meant I always had a place to live or return to if destitute. One of the greatest gimmicks was to produce slot machines that looked like gumball machines, and you can imagine the elation of a Catholic priest who put in his nickel and got a handful of coins. He exclaimed, "This is better than turning water into wine!"

Another trick of heavenly origin was that if a con was convicted, then his corrupt physician would extol the concept that the patient was in his "last throws," and then somehow the charges would be minimized but usually dropped as the half-deceased body would be removed from the hospital with resurrection occurring a day or two afterword.

White Sulphur Springs, West Virginia was the home of the Greenbrier, a magnificent facility in itself. I actually visited the Greenbrier after it became a headquarters for Jesuit priests – what a great way to fly. I often wondered how the Jesuits got such a joint, and bless their little hearts, it came through the Cleveland Syndicate, a religious organization of itself. Greenbrier was sure a lot closer than Hot Springs, Arkansas, and the pool at Greenbrier could be made as hot as one would wish, depending on the company you are keeping. One could even buy a drink in the contained Old White Glove of the Greenbrier, and thereby get around the state law of the single drink rule.

Well, guess who had been the first frontier of the Greenbrier in an effort to produce a gambling mecca? Remember the Van Sweringen brothers, who gave the real estate empire of Shaker Heights to Aunt Kitty? – Well, they were the ones who made the donation when they could no longer afford to keep the place going. Nor did it materialize as the gambling mecca which was originally conceived. The Van Boys had bought the Chesapeake and Ohio Railroad to ship booze around the northeast part of America. The business venture failed and the Van Sweringen brothers dumped a ton of money into the Greenbrier, which was again one of their ventures that failed. The Syndicate had considered building a major casino next to the Greenbrier, but at the last minute the whole deal fell through, thereby the Jesuits inherited the magnificent donation. With the Greenbrier concept out of the way, the Syndicate switched to the Desert Inn in Las Vegas, and along with the Rat Pack got that joint going.

Chapter Eighteen

The Syndicate had two casino robberies to deal with. One was a major heist of patrons and a safe at the Mounds Club in Lake County, Ohio in 1947 when I was 17 years old, and the second a smaller deal at the Continental Club. The Syndicate sought no assistance in the solution to the problem, but I will state that all of the robbers involved were dead within six months, and this was called "therapy." For some reason, no more robberies of Syndicate casinos occurred.

Many rumors abounded about the mechanism of execution of the robbers of those two casinos, but the two stories that I enjoyed the most were as follows:

It became known, through a squealer, that one of the guys was living in a treehouse outside of Bath, Ohio. Allegedly two vans pulled up to the property and the first had loud speakers on the top and the second no windows. While music from the speakers blared out the song "Pennies from Heaven," two guys with machine guns got out of the second van and sprayed the bottom of the treehouse with many bursts. Then they got back into the van, the music stopped, and off they drove into the blue, never to be seen again. A neighbor ran over and reported blood coming out of some of the holes in the floor of the treehouse.

The second therapy session occurred in the warehouse district of Cleveland and was even more amusing in that the robber saw the guys get out of the van with the machine guns, and he ran around the corner and into the trunk of a car. The problem was that one of the executioners saw the flight out of the corner of his eye, and multiple shots of the machine guns were fired and hit every segment of the closed trunk into which the robber was hiding. After the spray deal, both guys left without even opening the trunk and this maneuver was classified as an "air conditioning job," and I don't think that the boys belonged to the electrical union.

Political contributions to select individuals were the mechanism of obtaining early parole on several convicted lieutenants. Things in Washington haven't changed a bit, since even today lobbyists use the same mechanism to favor their clients with perhaps the pharmaceutical industry at the top of the list.

Harry Truman actually did a first-class cleanup job in Washington, especially in the Departments of Veteran Affairs and the IRS. Does this sound familiar with the new veteran hospital scandals and the recent issues with the IRS? The investigations and castigations continued until 1954.

The Syndicate next directed its attention to Las Vegas, where it gave Bugsy Siegel big bucks to build the Flamingo Hotel. This was a brilliant idea at the right time with the growing population of Los Angeles looking for a place to dump their money, and the Syndicate was more than willing to assist and cooperate in any and all ventures. Right about this time the Second World War ended, and Roosevelt died with the reins going to Harry Truman. The question was, "What would an honest man do in the White House?"

The Eastern Syndicate was maturing at this point in time, and they were concentrating on TV production and sales, anticipating that bars and taverns would be the primary market for such products. Private homes were simply not considered a priority and the whole move was secondary to the Syndicate's experience with jukeboxes, so the move to television was reasonable and logical.

Getting back to Jack Dragna, he had become the Al Capone of Los Angeles, and apparently he was never a part of the inner circle which made his longevity very precarious. The cops of L.A. were onto Dragna and his apartment was bugged. Word got out about the bugging and the rest of the underworld thought it was very humorous and that destroyed Dragna's power and relationship with the Boys, who were much more cautious and sophisticated. Remember, the Cleveland

Guys were smart and the gangsters in the rest of the country functioned at a far lesser level.

Dragna was classified as a Mafia leader but one would never know it by listening to copies of his recorded phone calls. Even I, as an amateur, know that the telephone is not the way to conduct "business." When Bugsy Siegel got bumped off, it took Lou Rothkopf over a year to get the California scene straightened out. Frank Costello assisted in the spiritual revival.

The Desert Inn became a main focus of distribution of the various ownerships when its success far exceeded the Flamingo. I have a shirt-sleeve relative who lost a ton of money at the Desert Inn, so I feel akin to the blood on the desert floor.

The first efforts to build the Desert Inn failed for lack of funding, and it was not until the Cleveland Syndicate did a transfusion that the construction continued and was completed. In Nevada, gambling was legal and it was like opening the gates to heaven, and it gave the Syndicate the opportunity to finally come out of the shadows and build an empire and to kick ass. Making money was a compulsion of the Boys and they made an art of it. The operation had previously been covert and shady, but now the shade was up and one could look into the window, and what you could see would fill a book in itself. At no time did the Syndicate become as bold and divisive as the Pink Panthers of Europe today. The PP's are the epitome of intelligence and diabolical planning plus boldness in the international world of crime.

The Kefauver committee was considered a "pain in the ass" by the Syndicate, and in reality convictions could always be lessened or eliminated, depending upon who you knew and how much you were willing to pay. The Nevada Tax Commission had to decide between honest respectability and profit, and you can guess which way they went. Everyone was a crook during prohibition, so the subsequent era consisted of the art of cleaning your own underwear or at least making it smell that way.

I was 20 years old when the big bucks went from Cleveland to the Desert Inn. I was studying like mad in college at the time so that I would not be drafted into that ridiculous Korean War, as three of my buddies had already been killed, so I knew very little of what was going on in Las Vegas at the time. The reason that the money for the Desert Inn was so readily obtained from all the Boys and their cronies was due to the fact that any and all wanted to appear legitimate in a state where gambling was permitted, and it worked.

The Harry Potter of Beverly Hills Kentucky Corporation obviously had nothing to do with the superstar Harry Potter of today's literature, but I'll bet he would have had a lot of fun playing the part. Actually, Potter came from Cleveland and had been a peasant in the earlier gambling traps and was used as a front in several of the schemes that kept the Feds on tranquilizers. He was a tool of the Syndicate that had the ability to use individuals in unique positions that were very difficult to define by the Feds or other investigators. The ability of the Syndicate to work together as a unit was unparalleled in the American underworld history, and this again was the reason for their continued success.

As the old geezers aged, a new generation of their college trained kids appeared on the horizon, and I knew several of them. As mentioned before, Angelo Milano, from Italy, and the nephew of Frank would pick me up on Sunday night at the corner of Chestnut Boulevard and State Road and we would drive to John Carroll University, which he attended for a year. He was actually by osmosis my ticket to events to come.

Although, supposedly, my mother and Aunt Kitty did not drink alcohol, alcoholism was very prevalent in the rest of the family and produced disasters at every turn in the road. My education in alcoholism was early and very simple in that my mother was the secretary to Sister Ignatia, the nun who founded Alcoholics Anonymous at the St. Thomas Hospital in Akron, Ohio. The lesson that I carried to this day were the words of Sister Ignatia herself, who told me that alcoholism is not determined by the volume of consumption but rather by the "level of importance" of the substance in an individual's life.

I was in high school during a major portion of the Second World War, and that truly had an effect on my thinking and planning. I had actually wanted to go to

West Point and be a pilot (before the days of the Air Force) but in those days you couldn't wear glasses and be accepted at West Point, so I turned my attention to the Coast Guard Academy at New London, Connecticut where I could be both a pilot and a sailor, but the war ended and I switched to medicine. To this day I regret not going into the Coast Guard.

Chapter Nineteen

One of the greatest investors in the Desert Inn was Frank Milano to the tune of one-half million bucks. Can you imagine what that would be in today's money market? Even though the money came from Mexico, I don't think it was in pesos. The Nevada Tax Commission had no idea as to where the money came from and Milano's investment was a very covert operation.

When Senator Estes Kefauver's committee went into full swing, this was the first coordinated effort by the Feds to get a handle on things. The committee was actually remarkable during the short time that it functioned, but how could you stop a rolling giant boulder, and they couldn't. Some of the most valuable records of the Syndicate miraculously disappeared and nobody had any idea where they went. Fortunately for the Syndicate, nothing of significance was ultimately found and even less was proven to be of any value. The United States attorney in Cleveland was Don Miller, and if that name sounds familiar it's because he had been one of the Four

Horseman of Notre Dame and was the brother of Ray Miller, the former mayor of Cleveland, and lifelong friend of my uncle Ray Lamb, who ended up being the finance director of the City of Cleveland (see, it pays to have friends – particularly in a cozy relationship).

The Cleveland Police were close mouthed to any and all investigations, and the old timers were quite familiar with my family members and knew that they could be counted upon for various legitimate activities, when needed. The cops continued to respect and call Aunt Kitty "Mrs. Logan," as they knew who the hell she was.

Information on the Syndicate Boys was simply not available, especially if one wished to live a long life. I must admit that my thinking and education via the Syndicate over the years definitely had an effect upon my fearless and brainless personality. Ultimately Ohio was classified as the Capital of the Underworld in America, and history has shown that to be correct. The Kefauver investigations were completely unsuccessful in nailing the big guys, and it became obvious over the years that Dalitz and Tucker were geniuses who were able to keep the confusion going and were never really nailed by the Feds.

My uncle Ray Lamb was supposed to be interviewed by the Kefauver committee, but Federal Attorney Don Miller found an escape hatch. Lying was an art and was considered a fact of life, and he used it. I had to purge myself of that mode of thinking and I was able to do so with a strong soap-suds enema, as I knew that form of functioning was simply not compatible with a professional life. I must admit, the results of the enema were effective. Even the judges were paid off (so what else is new) and I personally knew a judge in Summit County (Akron) who boasted that he could be had – and he was. The public saw the whole Kefauver thing as entertainment rather than justice and that is why the Committee lost its steam. You know steam does evaporate, and so do farts, including some of the ones that I knew.

The racetracks in Kentucky, plus the associated gambling casinos produced a myriad of arrests and minor convictions, most of which were dismissed in lieu of Mickey Mouse fines. The emphasis on racing and gambling switched from Kentucky to Tucson in about 1953, nine years before I hit the scene as a U.S. Army medical officer at Fort Huachuca, 90 miles southeast of Tucson. Although I had an invitation to visit the Boys at the Ranch, I kept my nose and butt clean and devoted all of my energies to my job, which was 24/7 but I did meet two of the Boys on one occasion at Licavoli's Ranch. They were behind the development of the Rillito Racetrack, but I never had the time to go there.

Chapter Twenty

Another investor in the Desert Inn was Barry Goldwater. I got in trouble with him at Fort Huachuca when a draftee, whose father owned a large grocery chain in California and was a major Goldwater contributor, decided to choke me to death in the hospital emergency department after he'd been brought in by two MP's because he had been eating cups out of the Coke machine (now figure that one out – he wanted to get out of the Army, one way or another). Well, the two MP's decided to get lunch and left the kid with me, and when my back was turned he jumped up and tried to choke me and was almost successful until I hit him in the balls and grabbed an iron bar which was holding the window open in the cantonment style building, and I made the immediate decision not to kill him but instead broke both of his collarbones with the metal bar, and he stood there crying with both arms hanging limp. I pushed the alarm button and all hell broke loose. The kid's father was on the phone to Senator Goldwater and I was in deep shit. I ultimately went to my secret problem solver, Mrs. Urhanne, the general's wife, and she took care of everything, and that is a story in itself.

In any case, Barry Goldwater had made a deal with Moe Dalitz to put his clothing store into the Desert Inn. My present wife was a frequent flyer in that clothing store, which changed its name to Distinctive Apparel so that when Goldwater ran for president of the United States it wouldn't look like he had a connection with the Gang or Syndicate. So you can see that it's not only the gangsters that changed their names, but even some of our honorable politicians.

There were three pioneer casinos in the United States. The first was the Thomas Club in Cleveland, followed by the Beverly Hills in Kentucky (not California), but the first big smash was the Desert Inn in Las Vegas. Just think, a state that permitted gambling. The Boys could now come out of the dungeons and caves and let the sun shine on their faces (actually not a pretty sight). The Desert Inn was the springboard of the development of a myriad of other enterprises in Las Vegas. Even accessory industries up to 100 miles surrounding Las Vegas sprung up and prospered like long-lost tulips seeking the air and sunlight of the now open Nevada.

Nevada literally exploded in growth with the Cleveland Syndicate behind most of the ventures. When a little extra dough was needed, the Syndicate contacted the Teamsters union back home under the fearless leadership of Jimmy Hoffa, and the request was honored. The growth of gambling in Las Vegas was overwhelming and it looked like Cleveland all over again but in a concentrated perspective, as the gambling became the primary focus of Las Vegas. Actually, the growth far exceeded the limitations and expectations of both Cleveland and Ohio.

The Desert Inn was the most stable of all the enterprises, and again, the leadership could be traced back to Dalitz, the genius. Only one of the originals stayed in the Cleveland area, and that was Lou Rothkopf, who lived outside Chagrin Falls. Lou eventually became severely depressed and committed suicide, and that was very rare amongst the original Syndicate team. With Rothkopf out of the way, Tommy McGinty (the mysterious Russian) stepped forward.

Another suicide occurred in 1959 when top dog "Longie" Zwillman killed himself, and this was a major blow to the Eastern Syndicate, where the focus was still on participating in the Las Vegas venture. The death of Zwillman literally dealt the Boys in the Eastern Syndicate out of the Las Vegas prosperity.

The Stardust Hotel and Casino got into the show business and that put the profits ahead of the Desert Inn. Ed Sullivan, of TV fame, was the show at the Stardust for four weeks, and rumor had it that he also had real estate connections in the hotel with the Cleveland Syndicate. The super show that followed Sullivan was Lido de Paris, and that allowed the loose standards of Nevada to show boobs and butts in abundance from all angles.

Chapter Twenty-One

The next character to step forward was Meyer Lansky, who decided to develop the Havana connection. His relationship to the Nacional Hotel was quite successful until the war put a crimp on things and the casino business in Cuba fell off the road, even though Lansky and Batista were good friends. Instead, Lansky returned to Florida where he rejoined his old buddies from the Eastern Syndicate in many developments, but they never matched the ingenuity and scope of the Cleveland Syndicate.

The Kefauver investigation strangled the "joints" in Florida and Lansky looked again toward Cuba. His old buddy Batista was in the "outs" and was living in Florida. Money from the Eastern Syndicate and assistance from the Cuban army enabled Batista to regain power and return to Havana. Behind the entire transition back to Cuba for Batista was the Cuban communist party. This produced problems in the American/Cuban relationship. Sugar was still a big deal but Cuba needed tourists and gambling was the way to get them. Thus the world-famous Riviera Hotel was built and the old Nacional Hotel was taken over by the Cleveland Syndicate, the masters of developing profits.

The closest I got to Cuba was, not by choice, in that I was in the U.S. Army and stationed at Fort Huachuca, Arizona in the early 1960s when we got word that we were going to invade Cuba, since the Bay of Pigs safari was a total disaster. Along with other preparations, I received 14 shots in my outer thighs (that was the Army's way of giving shots) and I could hardly walk for two days. Well, we made all the preparations but were never deployed. I still have in use my old Army Castro cap to work in the garden, so at least I got some benefit from the whole situation.

My only other Cuban experience was that on two occasions I was the assistant bartender at private parties of Xavier Cugat, the renowned Cuban band leader, at his home in the Edgewater Beach Apartments in Chicago on the North Shore Drive. A classmate in medical school was the head bartender and I was the go-fer. The parties were actually great to watch, and Cugat had a girlfriend and singer named Abbey Lane (wow) and she had a little dog that she carried around all the time. After she had a few drinks, she was able to produce a remarkable striptease, to the amusement of the entire party. I must admit that I was one of the observers.

Pan American Airways had a subsidiary in Havana called the Intercontinental Hotels Corporation and by that mechanism they developed a casino in Havana, and since the organization was international in scope, they could move money in and out of Cuba with less red tape. Also, to get around U.S. income taxes, a holding company in Panama was developed and that also eliminated the requirement of an annual audit. To further confuse the Feds, the profits ended up in two banks in America, one in Miami Beach and the other in Newark, New Jersey. Funds from the Union National Bank in Newark were used to develop a huge housing project in Philadelphia (who said that the Boys were not philanthropic?).

Funneling money from three international casinos to one account made it possible to skim dough off the top (another stroke of genius). There is also an art of taking money off the top before an accounting is done and the mechanisms of avoiding taxation were ingenious. Foreign holding companies didn't have to account to anyone or anything, and therefore the cash generated at the casinos in Havana experienced a dancing merry-go-round as it bounced back and forth across the border and into various banks and pockets. The tricks were endless and very profitable and the entire operation was called "black money," and the same system, with modifications, is used today with even countries like Switzerland getting into the act and the game, and that continues to exist up to the present time.

As an additional complicating factor, the United States was selling military equipment to Batista, hoping to foment a collapse of the communist party. Batista subsequently fled the nation and then America was supposed to back up the Bay of Pigs fiasco, which had failed miserably. America should have had a clear signal that Cuba was ripe for communism back in 1958 based on a report of the Cuban National Council. American politicians were either totally blind or had self interests in Cuba that prevented realistic insight into the problem.

In spite of the total mess in Cuba, the only organization that really functioned in a coordinated and intelligent fashion in dealing with the various factions within Cuba was the Cleveland Syndicate. At the appropriate time they reasoned that a bailout was the most reasonable approach but they needed a sucker buyer in the process. Believe it or not, they picked the Nevada Tax Commission as their victim in the sale and the Commission literally had their mouths open and their brains shut when they agreed to the purchase. After Batista fled Cuba and the entire operation collapsed, the buyers were left on the hook and the Syndicate again came out smiling and profitable.

The next site of activity was Haiti. Remember "Papa" Duvalier? If you think poverty was bigtime in Cuba, you should visit Haiti. I worked temporarily as a surgeon in the Dominican Republic, adjacent to Haiti, and literally gave up since I couldn't get anything done within any reasonable period of time. The only thing I learned in my brief stay was that I didn't need screens on the windows and instead I had six chameleons in the apartment who kept the joint clean from flies and insects.

The task of exploring Haiti went to Meyer Lansky. The Cleveland Syndicate explored all the options and chose not to bite, another wise decision. So the emphasis went back to Cuba, and at this time Fidel Castro was top dog and the revolution was on the move. Gambling was permitted temporarily but could not last with no visitors because of the revolution.

So the Boys who profited by booze-running were still going full tilt in the '60s with merely a change in the venue, but there were plenty of problems. If you remember George Ratterman, the football player for the Cleveland Browns, he headed a cleanup movement and was elected sheriff of Newport, Kentucky and was literally backed by all segments of the local society in Newport. Campbell County got cleaned up, however, fraud prevailed and Ratterman was allegedly drugged and photographed in a most compromising situation. However, the community saw through the scam and exonerated Ratterman and the purgation of corruption resumed.

The joints closed and Newport became a ghost town. That's okay if you like ghosts, but they don't produce jobs except on Halloween night. New industry moved into the area with the closing of gambling, but it took a long time and federal assistance for Newport to get its head above water.

The Big Boys continued to develop Las Vegas and spread internationally, giving up on some of the smaller and less profitable sites. Radio and TV stations became the new vista and my relatives climbed onto the bandwagon in Cleveland, buying radio and starting TV stations plus moving on into trucking, a very successful business which continues to be run by my family up to the present time. My relatives were smart enough to develop regional trucking since over-the-road trucking was already a saturated entity. Although my family's trucking operations were completely legit, many other questionable sideline trucking businesses were developed. For example, Refrigerated Transport Company figured out a way to sell and transport slot machines to Germany. No wonder Hitler was upset.

If one wishes to criticize the Syndicate for tax evasion, please study the tactics of politicians in Washington D.C. today. We also have the significant problem of profitable American corporations moving their headquarters to other nations for the sole purpose of tax reduction and/or evasion. That practice continues up to the present time and overall it appears that the only segment of our society that has to toe the line on legitimate taxation and payments is the middle class of America. It does not take a mental giant to figure out that such a process is the inevitable road to disaster, and we are well on the way at the present time.

So who was the next person to come on the scene and function as the savior of America? As attorney general, Robert F. Kennedy attempted to do so, and look what happened to him and his brother. Who do you think engineered those assassinations? I don't really think it was a group of nuns. Do you have the answer? The underworld in America was really feeling heat from Robert Kennedy in his role of attorney general, and he actually was very astute in the process. Many other high-profile individuals in the process did not have either the ambition or insight to make changes in various segments and levels of national corruption which were not of the sophisticated level and productivity of the Syndicate.

Chapter Twenty-Two

It took the brilliance of J. Edgar Hoover to admit that there was a "Mafia" but he forgot to mention that it was a very spiritual organization, similar to the Dali Lama. The title of Cosa Nostra was the product of Joseph Valachi (so what's in a new name?). The Syndicate Boys, especially the lieutenants, would change their names on any passing impulse, particularly if it was of hormone origin.

Rumors of the Las Vegas development being a product of Chicago's underworld brilliance was total and complete fabrication. Maybe the Cleveland Syndicate wanted it to look that way – or look the other way. Somehow the La Cosa Nostra fiasco did not rub off on the Cleveland Syndicate but was probably a misdirected venture of hoods in New York who were nowhere near as organized and polished as the Cleveland Syndicate. Likewise, the Capone mob didn't hold a candle to the Cleveland Syndicate in terms of planning and getting the job done with minimal complications or side effects.

Back to the Cleveland scene, the Theatrical Restaurant had been rebuilt after the fire into a magnificent structure, and even by 1965 was the Syndicate's headquarters. That was the span during which I was playing doctor in Minneapolis, actually an orthopedic traumatologist, simon-pure in all aspects.

A coffee shop in Miami was a key communication center and much business was provided over a bagel, both regionally and nationally, and also extending into the Caribbean. It is not unusual to have covert business conducted in small food shops or restaurants. The Theatrical Restaurant in Cleveland was an example but of a much grander scale. The concept reminds me of one of my foolish ventures that occurred when I was medical director of a hospital in Harrisburg, Pennsylvania in 1990. One of my unpaid civic duties in Harrisburg was that of being chairman of the board of health of the city. The biggest plus of the task was that I was able to park in the mayor's spot when conducting the meetings in the downtown office building. The full-time health inspector informed me of a "quick chicken shop," where upon request, a buyer would state that the "special chicken" was requested. I was then informed of the content of the "special chicken" and therefore made the magnificent decision to hit the joint on a Saturday morning with two cops, the full-time inspector and myself after getting another plainclothes cop to function as the buyer and request the "special chicken." Sure enough, under the chicken, separated by a neatly folded napkin, was the cocaine. The whole deal was done covertly and even the chief hospital administrator did not find out about my participation. My diabolical mind had worked again.

So what do I wish that each reader would learn from this book? – Namely that four men, Dalitz, Kleinman, Rothkopf and Tucker, the founders of the Cleveland Syndicate, were four of the most intelligent men in American history and their tactics were no different than those used today in American business and politics, with much less success. It is so easy to criticize others but one must understand the good that was derived from the efforts of these men, not only in the City of Cleveland but throughout the nation, considering not only the employment that they afforded to the immigrants and middle class, but also the actual development of certain areas of the country, such as Las Vegas. These men were the prototypes for progress not only with the vision but also the capability of carrying out those concepts and visions. Please compare their efforts and accomplishments with our government of today, where neither legal nor ethical principles are pursued or followed. I will always have great admiration for those four individuals and their families who did so much for both Cleveland and our nation and also provided employment for my own family.

Oh, by the way, I spent 14 months in Rainbow Hospital in South Euclid, Ohio (a suburb of Cleveland), being sent there at age nine and allegedly "supposed to die," and it was a member of the Cleveland Syndicate who paid the entire bill. No more needs be said.

The End